PUT YOUR
BUSINESS
ON
AUTOPILOT

T0165731

PUT YOUR
BUSINESS
ON
AUTOPILOT

SMART STRATEGIES
TO OPTIMIZE YOUR BUSINESS

GEORGE MAABADI
PRESIDENT & CEO OF THE GROWTH COACH SAN DIEGO

DANIEL MURPHY
FOUNDER & CEO OF THE GROWTH COACH

Published by Advantage, Charleston, South Carolina.
Member of Advantage Media Group.

ADVANTAGE is a registered trademark and the Advantage colophon is a trademark of Advantage Media Group, Inc.

Printed in the United States of America.

ISBN: 978-159932-575-0
LCCN: 2014959580

This publication is designed to provide accurate and authoritative information in regard to the subject matter covered. It is sold with the understanding that the publisher is not engaged in rendering legal, accounting, or other professional services. If legal advice or other expert assistance is required, the services of a competent professional person should be sought.

Advantage Media Group is proud to be a part of the Tree Neutral® program. Tree Neutral offsets the number of trees consumed in the production and printing of this book by taking proactive steps such as planting trees in direct proportion to the number of trees used to print books. To learn more about Tree Neutral, please visit **www.treeneutral.com**. To learn more about Advantage's commitment to being a responsible steward of the environment, please visit **www.advantagefamily.com/green**

Advantage Media Group is a publisher of business, self-improvement, and professional development books and online learning. We help entrepreneurs, business leaders, and professionals share their Stories, Passion, and Knowledge to help others Learn & Grow. Do you have a manuscript or book idea that you would like us to consider for publishing? Please visit **advantagefamily.com** or call **1.866.775.1696**.

This book is dedicated to the millions of small business owners, franchisees, and self-employed professionals throughout the world desiring greater financial success, freedom, and fun. With the right changes in mindset and habits, you can break free from feeling overworked, overwhelmed, frustrated, or like a prisoner to your business.

FOREWORD

You are holding this book because you want to get more out of your business and life. You have found the right resource. This practical book is intended to help drive the success and balance the lives of small business owners, franchisees, managers, and self-employed professionals. The proven process set forth in this book will help you take your business to a higher level.

This book is also for people who feel overworked, overwhelmed and like prisoners to their businesses. It's for owners experiencing more frustration than fun, more isolation than satisfaction. If you are overly busy and exhausted, this book will help you to slow down, reflect, face reality and determine the critical changes you need to make to improve your business and personal life.

The good news is you *can* achieve greater freedom, fulfillment, financial success and peace of mind; however, for your business and personal life to change, **you must change!** You must think and act differently by reevaluating your business and your roles —both professional and personal—in sum, your current life. In order to fall in love with your business again, to reignite your drive and passion for your business, **you** will have to adopt a strategic mindset and focused approach to running your company. Our proven process will help guide you there.

TABLE OF CONTENTS

INTRODUCTION

Almost all quality improvement comes via simplification
of design, manufacturing... layout, processes, and procedures.
TOM PETERS

As a small business owner, you know all too well how precious your time is. Even when you are not at work, you are thinking about how you need to get more done. It is probably one of your first thoughts when you wake up and one of the last things on your mind before you fall asleep.

It is time to ask yourself some tough questions about how you spend your time. Honestly, when was the last time you had a work-free, guilt-free vacation? If you got sick tomorrow, would your business survive without you for a week? If your business were for sale today in its current condition, would you be a willing buyer?

If you answered "No" or "Never" to any of these questions, it means your business is not properly structured or systematized to run on autopilot without you, and that is a one-way ticket to disaster.

A lot of business owners today are consumed with doing clever things that are definitely not the right things. Believe it or not, doing things "100% right" is not necessarily the most effective way. It is making sure you are doing the right things to produce superior results rather than doing the wrong things right. You have to make sure that you are working on relationships with key customers, but also your relationships with your family, friends, and your community.

Okay, let me be very clear. Regardless of your industry, **you should not be chained to your business**. It should serve you and give you *greater* freedom and more time, not less.

In fact, when it is properly designed, your business should be able to run on autopilot for days without your being there to handle the day-to-day problems. Your business, not you, should work harder. It should be systems dependent—not owner dependent—for its success.

It is important to take a step back and look at what is happening. If everything in your business depends on you, then you are dramatically restricting its growth and profit potential. There are limits to the amount of work, number of transactions, problems, and decisions that one human being can effectively handle in a given day. Stop making yourself crazy and missing out on greater personal freedom, money, and happiness.

I know what it is like. I have spent over 30 years in sales, marketing, coaching, and mentoring for Fortune 500 companies including IBM, Novell, and SCO. I have also owned a software development company, an Internet-based company, and a construction company. Early on, I was eager to work extra hours and help my business grow, but when it did, I had more and more to do. Delegating was tricky because I could not let go, and sometimes because I had the wrong employees.

The way businesses market and sell today is completely different than it used to be when I started over 30 years ago. And it is getting harder every day. With the advances in technology coming faster and faster, there is a huge amount of information that buyers can get their hands on now before they even meet a vendor. You really need to be able to leverage marketing and educate the public on what you have to offer before you can start selling. If you are not careful, you can quickly get frustrated and overwhelmed.

When that happens, it is easy to get into a reactive mode all of the time and just work "in" your business. If you learn how to step back a little, you can get into a proactive mode where you can set goals, develop a vision and start working "on" your business. The only way your company will really thrive is if you learn to identify your priorities and begin to delegate. It often requires somebody who has been in your position to help you get on the right track.

That is where we come in. At The Growth Coach San Diego, we are passionate about helping business owners, executives, and professionals like you clarify your business direction, increase your results, and find that all-important balance between work and family life.

By building the right structures and systems, you will be able to enjoy work more, work fewer hours, and actually make your company worth more if you decide to sell it in the future. It is probably the last thing on your mind, but by doing these things now, you will not only sleep better, but you will be able to sell your business down the road for much more than it is currently worth.

To do it, you will need to start thinking about how to systemize what you do and make sure that the "autopilot button" works as soon as possible. Over 90 percent of small businesses in this country are not reaching their potential value because they are owner dependent. Your business will have a higher value if it can run itself without you. So the idea is to start learning the right skills, getting in the right mindset, and developing the right systems today whether you want to sell it today or twenty years from now or pass it on to your heirs. The longer you wait, the more your business will grow to depend on you and the more tired, frustrated, and overwhelmed you will become.

If you have been in business for three years, you have three employees or more and you have revenues between $300,000 and

$20 million, this book could be for you. If you sometimes feel like a prisoner or slave to your business or struggle to manage its growing size and complexity, this book probably is for you. If you wish to be more effective, work less, and make more money, this book definitely is for you.

This book also should be mandatory for your current or future advisers and coaches. These professionals cannot help you if they do not understand your real issues and challenges or the strategic solutions that are available. The Growth Coach San Diego coaches have been professionally trained and certified in our ongoing coaching and accountability process and genuinely understand the strategic solutions addressed in this book.

Honestly, this book is not intended for entrepreneurs with a business still in diapers—in the start-up phase. They are still babies, in a sense. No disrespect, but such proud owners are still running on the passion, promises, and adrenaline associated with a newborn enterprise. They are generally are too busy to be coached at this point. Starting out, they accept the 12-hour workdays, being chained to the business, and are intoxicated by the details of a new venture. The few wise enough to start shaping their businesses while still in the nursery, however, will avoid many growing pains and headaches down the road. The sooner you adopt a strategic mindset, the better.

Consider the following metaphor—creating a baby is rather easy and enjoyable; raising a child is much more challenging. Similarly, starting a business is fairly simple and fun; managing a growing and complex business is much more difficult. As such, this book was written for owners who feel like hostages to their businesses, are overwhelmed by growing complexities, and are wondering what the heck they got themselves into.

If you feel compelled to control and do everything in your business yourself or if you are starting to question and reexamine your life, priorities and personal sacrifices, this resource can serve as a formula for freedom.

The Growth Coach Strategic Mindset Process is exactly the right tool for business owners. It is different because it was specifically developed by small business owners to help other small business owners slow down, reflect, and map out the critical changes necessary to shape better businesses and better lives. Most other coaching companies do not have tools like these. This book, combined with a series of in-person workshops, outlines a system that will help you with the tools to be a smarter business owner of a more efficient company. It is only through transforming your mindset, behavior and habits that you can achieve and sustain superior results.

Let us be very clear—you are the expert in your business and industry; we are not and will never claim to be. Our expertise is in guiding business owners to unlock their greater potential by helping them enhance their strategic mindset, focus, actions and results.

You will find that there is so much to learn that you will want to read the book several times. And then, if there is a specific issue you are solving at your business, you will know where to turn for a refresher. Our mission is well defined: Driving Success. Balancing Life.® We can help guide you to become more effective, focused, and productive. The powerful and proven process described in this book allows you to see the big picture and go to work "on" your business.

To reinforce the book's concepts, the Growth Coach provides guidance on strategic selling, marketing, leadership, and people management. Each quarter, the strategically focused projects build on the concepts in the book and provide proven, customized action plans to ensure that you are ready to move your business to the next level.

The Growth Coach San Diego even goes one step further. We provide one-on-one accountability sessions before and after each quarterly workshop to customize your learning to your specific business needs. These sessions provide the opportunity to discuss private issues that are affecting your business. They also give you a chance to implement ideas and set monthly deadlines to get faster results. These private sessions could take 60 to 90 minutes, depending on your needs, and conducting them is a commitment we have made to each of our business owners since opening our office here in San Diego in 2011.

We truly are on a mission to educate you and help your business to grow.

Do you consider yourself a strategic business owner—someone who gets the highest and best return possible for your time, money, and effort? Ask yourself the following questions:

- Have you achieved any of the things that motivated you to start your own business?

- Do you think more like a CEO than an employee?

- Do you create an annual business plan?

- Do you focus on your entire business rather than its daily technical operations?

- Have you created systems and policies to help operate your company?

- Have you developed and documented all your key business processes?

- Have you created a systems-dependent business instead of an owner-dependent business?

- Do you spend more time on important strategic matters than on trivial/urgent matters?

- Do you conduct one-on-one monthly coaching sessions with your managers and/or key employees?

- Do you avoid getting buried in the day-to-day details and headaches of the business?

- Have you shaped your business more by design than by default?

- Are you experiencing more fun and fulfillment than frustrations?

If you answered "No" to more than three of these questions you can definitely benefit from this book and the Growth Coach system.

Be warned, this is not just a one-time homework assignment—it is going to take some work to learn and to sustain. Going forward, you will have to change your mindset.

In addition, you have to be coachable. If you are not willing to take the time and put in the effort to do the work, then you are wasting your time and money. Take professional athletes, for example. It does not make a difference how many coaches they have, if they are not ready to put in the effort, success will not happen.

The bottom line is that if you want better results, you have to take different steps. It is time to get out of your comfort zone and learn to let go. We are here to point you in the right direction. To do that, however, you need to change your mindset from whatever you are doing today that is not working. You need to learn more about yourself and your business by facing reality.

Turn down the ego and admit that something is broken. Be honest with yourself, reflect and refocus your energy. Stop treating the symptoms and get to the root causes. Be prepared to deconstruct and rebuild your business and management approach to achieve long-term solutions to your hassles and headaches.

Regardless of how frazzled and swamped you may feel, know that there is hope for real relief. Your past does not have to equal your future. Whether you have three employees or 1,000, there are practical solutions to gain more freedom, flexibility, and fulfillment in your life. The answer is not to shift into higher gear, it is to shift mindsets. Sustained relief comes from changing mindsets and strategies, not gears. To gain a fresh start, you need to reboot your mental software and adopt new attitudes and strategic approaches.

This book will help you adjust your mindset and habits in order to transform your business and life for the better. This educational journey will allow you to redesign your business and regain your personal life and freedom. While we cannot promise total enlightenment, we are confident that this book will help you map out your path to progress.

George Bernard Shaw stated, "Progress is impossible without change, and those who cannot change their minds cannot change anything." We hope to share valuable lessons and insights with you that will help you change and rediscover the joy, passion, and freedom of being a business owner.

George Maabadi
thegrowthcoachsandiego.com

Enhancing the strategic mindset, focus and results of small business owners, franchisees, managers, and the self-employed.

CHAPTER 1

FACE REALITY

POINTS TO PONDER

Honesty is the first chapter of the book of wisdom.
THOMAS JEFFERSON

Nothing about ourselves can be changed until it is first accepted.
SHELDON KOPP

The first and best victory is to conquer self.
PLATO

ENTREPRENEURIAL REFLECTION

Not everything that is faced can be changed, but nothing can be changed until it is faced.

For many of us, in as few as two to three years (and regardless of the level of financial success we've achieved), our entrepreneurial dream of freedom, independence and wealth has warped into a waking nightmare. Our quest to be masters of our destinies has made us into slaves to our businesses, our employees and our customers. The fire in our bellies has been replaced by a growing uneasiness in our guts.

Habitually, we are still working too many hours, wearing too many hats, and handling too many things. Sadly, the entrepreneurial lows have become deeper, last longer and are more frequent. As our businesses have grown, our fun and fulfillment have deteriorated. In fact, we're likely to suffer from feelings of anxiety, mental fatigue, and of being trapped in the business. We call these feelings **the business owner blues.**

For years, we've deluded ourselves into thinking we would one day get caught up, slow down, and have more free time—and that the blues would eventually fade. But the reality is that the 60-70 hour workweeks continue. The stress continues. We can't even escape the business for a few relaxing, no-work days. We still scramble like hyperactive squirrels preparing for a harsh winter.

We have realized that being workaholics, micro-managers, control freaks, dictators or hands-on technicians is a miserable way to run a business, much less lead a rewarding life. Working harder, acting tougher, or being more involved with daily details is not the path to greater freedom, joy and peace of mind; rather, it is a guaranteed path to burnout. But we can't seem to get off the treadmill.

How did we get to this point? Odds are, we started out as gifted technicians (programmers, electricians, painters, landscapers, CPAs, mechanics, chefs, attornies, carpenters, salespeople, etc.) who caught the "entrepreneurial bug" several years ago and created, acquired or inherited a business—one that probably mirrors those technical skills and experience. Now, as we frantically try to maintain control of our growing companies, we are likely overworked, overwhelmed and suffering from a full-blown case of the business owner blues. As our businesses grow, we work even harder and become more deeply enslaved. The work, the problems, and the company revolve around us.

Let's be honest—business ownership is probably quite different from what most of us expected or were prepared to handle. If not held in check, the very strengths that made us successful technicians (detail orientation, hands-on doer, technical expertise, day-to-day focus, etc.) can be real liabilities to us as business owners.

Technical expertise alone is never sufficient to build and manage a healthy and profitable business. We must provide the vision and leadership of a chief executive officer (CEO) and the order and systems of a manager. We must strategize to be free! We must learn to concentrate on the future of the entire business, not merely the daily technical operations. We must elevate our mindsets and actions to focus on the vital few things that will make a difference.

For example, being a great plumber is completely different than creating and operating a successful plumbing business. Each role presents its own challenges requiring very specific skills and mindsets. To be effective, the latter requires strategic leadership; the former requires technical "doer-ship." Just because you are an expert plumbing technician doesn't mean you're qualified to build and manage a successful plumbing business. This is a fatal assumption most entrepreneurs make.

If you are a technician masquerading as an owner, be warned: Your pipes may burst. You have the wrong perspective, and you are doing the wrong type of work. As your company grows, you will find yourself doing the majority of plumbing work out of habit—because that's what you are good at and comfortable with. Soon, you will get caught up in the frantic pace, and before you know it, your business will be holding you hostage. You will forever be trapped under the sink or hovering over a broken toilet. Why? Because your business is broken too! You are not thinking and functioning as a strategic business owner; you are toiling and sweating like a plumber.

TIME TO FACE FACTS

It is no accident that you are reading this book. Out of either inspiration or desperation, you are seeking alternative approaches to business and life. You can see that your current beliefs, habits and actions are not yielding the results you want. You desire greater success, peace of mind, and joy. You want to make a life that works for you, not make a living from your work, and to regain balance in your life.

But for change to occur, you must stop playing mind games and admit that something about your business is not working. While sacrificing long hours each week may have been necessary the first few years, continuation of such a frantic pace is symptomatic of deeper issues. We shouldn't have to live this way! Something is wrong. Something is off. You know it in your gut. Others probably sense it in your moods, or see the stress written plainly on your face.

It is time to face reality: Our businesses and we have problems that require solutions, and the first step is to openly acknowledge this fact. To begin the transformation and healing process, we need to do some serious reflection. Be brutally honest when you answer these questions:

- Do I often ask, "Why do I have to do every darn thing myself?"

- Am I still working too much and making too little?

- Am I trapped working "in" my business instead of "on" my business?

- Do I ever wonder if business ownership is truly worth the time, effort, headaches, hassles and sacrifices?

- Do I feel trapped on a treadmill, moving faster and faster, but going nowhere?

- Do I constantly face frequent interruptions and repetitive questions from my staff?

- Do I go home many nights feeling mentally and physically drained?

- Do I confuse busyness with accomplishment?

- Do I dread the drudgery of facing and solving the same issues and problems each and every day—the burden of re-creating the wheel again and again?

- Do I daydream about regaining my sense of freedom, joy, passion and peace of mind?

- Am I anxious about drowning in projects, problems, deadlines, crises, meetings, employee issues, unanswered voicemails/emails, customer complaints, and administrative trivia?

- Do I feel like a master juggler with too many balls in the air and dreading they will soon begin hitting the floor?

- Am I forever chained to a phone, computer, email or pager?

- Am I tired of having customers rely on me personally for services, solutions and satisfaction?

- Am I fed up with missing family time and family events, and making other personal sacrifices on a semi-regular basis?

- Do I crave more free time to do the things that matter most to me?

ADMIT THE PROBLEM

If you answered "yes" to most of these questions, don't feel guilty, ashamed or embarrassed. You are not alone. Most owners have never learned to be strategic. Role models are scarce. As such, dysfunctional businesses and owners are the rule, not the exception.

Like you, most owners feel that they have been sentenced to a life of servitude and some even suffer from the blues. Unfortunately, because of pride, shame or ignorance, this sad condition has been kept hidden in the corner office for too long. Through this book, it is time to unveil this entrepreneurial dirty secret.

We do not have to live this way. We should not be consumed by our businesses and frustrated with our lives. Stop and think— as the owner, why in the world should you have to touch every transaction, help make every decision and solve every problem? You shouldn't! It doesn't make sense. Something is broken. You cannot succeed alone. You don't have enough energy or hours in the day to do everything yourself. Pain is a good indication that something is damaged and needs to be repaired.

Let this book serve as your shock therapy. Realize that you aren't the only one suffering. Think about how your stress and blues are negatively impacting your employees, customers, vendors/suppliers, friends, and if applicable, your spouse and kids.

Hear this wake-up call; it is time to radically shift our business beliefs and behavior. It is time to expand our views of new possibilities for managing our businesses and lives. The better our businesses function, the better our lives will function.

We deserve to be free from the daily grind; after all, we own a business, not a job. We should actually enjoy the journey of developing and running a business and not defer our personal lives and happiness until we retire or sell. Live life now! Let's not get so caught up in making a living that we forget to make a life. If our personal lives are suffering because of our companies, either our leadership approaches are misguided or our business designs are broken; maybe both.

At this point, we must simply admit that our businesses revolve around and are totally dependent on us. Admit that we are buried up to our eyeballs in the details of our businesses. Admit that we are hostages to our businesses. Admit that, as our headaches and hassles grow, our freedom and spirits wane.

We need to accept and understand that the majority, if not all, of these problems stem from the fact that we are too focused on the day-to-day to see the big picture. To break free and become strategic business owners, we must adopt a strategic mindset, focus and approach to running our businesses and our lives. We must rise above to see the forest through the trees.

GET A COACH

What is necessary to change a person is to
change his awareness of himself.
ABRAHAM MASLOW

Over the years that we have worked with entrepreneurs, we've learned that people will not make the changes necessary to improve their lives and businesses unless they are held accountable. Everyone could benefit from a business coach or, better yet, a year-round coaching and accountability process that would help us to see and understand the truth about the impact of our outward and repeated behaviors.

Unfortunately, human nature is too subjective to allow for such objective self-evaluation and feedback. We judge our surroundings and ourselves by our inward perceptions of reality, which very often are mild distortions, if not complete illusions.

Even with this guidebook, you will not be able to achieve such a strategic transformation on your own. No significant and sustainable changes will occur without a real-world evaluation and accountability process. You will need additional coaching to achieve real and lasting breakthroughs. Even great athletes like Peyton Manning and Drew Brees need coaches to help elevate their thinking, talents and results.

We could all use an objective, caring coach who will challenge our old, limiting assumptions and monitor our progress; someone who will hold us to a higher standard of success and excellence, ask the tough questions and force us to slow down, reflect on and analyze our progress. A great coach will help us to define and achieve both our personal and professional goals.

A professional business coach will help you achieve this critical renewal of the mind. Conformity is your jailer; to break free, you must move away from typical business owner practices and beliefs. For maximum results, engage a dedicated business coach—someone who has a proven process to help you get more of what you want and less of what you don't.

To work with someone who knows the philosophy and methodology of this book inside and out, search out a small business coach affiliated with The Growth Coach®. They are professionally trained and certified in The Strategic Mindset Process®, our year-round coaching and accountability process. The quarterly strategic-focusing process is affordable, guaranteed, and will help you make the necessary transformations of mindset, habits and business strategies.

Regardless of the help you choose, be open and be coachable. Meet regularly with your coach, whether it be quarterly or monthly. Ask him or her to monitor your adoption and implementation of the philosophies, strategies and habits suggested in this book. The value of receiving candid, objective feedback on your progress during these accountability sessions cannot be overstated.

OTHER TIPS & SUGGESTIONS

The success system you're holding in your hands is a practical and no-nonsense guidebook that comes from the collective achievements, pain and lessons of others. The wisdom captured here emanates from our personal business successes and failures, along with the struggles and triumphs of the many clients we have served over the years.

Please understand there are no shortcuts or tricks contained in this book. You alone are the agent of change. You must discipline your mind so it doesn't automatically react in old, harmful, habitual ways. You must internalize and fully apply these ideas in a way that is unique to, and appropriate for, you and your business. Adopt and adapt.

Guard against the temptation to reflexively dismiss these ideas as "simple" and "obvious." As with most things in life, success is less about ideas and more about aggressive implementation. Knowing what to do and doing what you know are very different things. Your task is to consider carefully these ideas and then fully implement those that make sense for your business. Again, enlist the assistance of your accountability coach to achieve your goals!

For self-employed owners (soloists), you should begin to apply these strategies as you grow your business and add employees. Your challenge will be to define and document the different job functions you currently perform, and to eventually hire people to replace you in those technical roles. Even if you decide to remain solo, you can still benefit greatly from the strategic discussions on a CEO mindset, business system creation and documentation, leadership, business planning, marketing, people management, and learning to let go.

You'll see certain themes and ideas repeated throughout this book. These reiterations aren't accidental; they're based on a belief in the power of repetition to fundamentally change the way we think. Some new ideas need to be sown more than once before they'll take root. Studies show it takes three exposures to a new idea before it is learned, a fourth exposure to reinforce it, and a fifth to internalize it and own it. Embrace the repetition and don't fight it.

Make this book your own. Highlight key ideas and jot down main thoughts. Only when an idea is written down do you truly own it. Write down the philosophies and strategies you wish to implement.

Finally, judge this book on its effectiveness at transforming your mindset from that of a doer to a leader; from that of an employee to a CEO. If this book helps you become more strategic and proactive, we both will have succeeded, and you will be well on your way to more profits, joy, freedom and peace of mind.

Be realistic and patient with your transformation; you cannot change your mindset overnight. Stepping out of your comfort zone will take ongoing courage. You may have to take a step back to advance two. It will take time and help from your coach or a coaching process; don't get discouraged. The long-term joy will be worth the short-term discomfort and sacrifice.

The answers and wisdom you seek are already within you; this book will merely help release them if you are ready. Have the humility to keep an open mind, the willingness to change your mindset, the courage to unlearn some of your assumptions, and the resolve to take aggressive action on new ideas, philosophies and strategies.

SUGGESTED ACTION ITEMS:

- Admit to yourself that something is broken in the way you have designed your business. Resolve to take corrective action with the help from this book.

- As you read it, mark the heck out of this book—write down notes, highlight key concepts, etc. Go back and underline key revelations. Make this book your own.

- After reading each chapter, take aggressive action on Suggested Action Items appropriate to your situation. Jot down your own to-do list as well.

- Commit to finishing this book within 30 days. Share this pledge with a key person in your life. Give that person a firm date 30 days out by which you will be finished. In 15 days, have him or her contact you in order to gauge your progress. Encourage them to kick your butt if necessary.

- Insist each of your key business advisers reads this book to foster a common understanding and vocabulary of the process needed to improve your business and your personal life. If they aren't willing to partner with you in this important journey, consider getting new advisers.

- As with most things in life, success is less about ideas and more about aggressive implementation. Knowing what to do and doing what you know are very different things. Select an accountability coach within the next 21 days. Choose someone you trust to hold you accountable for objectively reviewing your business and personal life and for making the changes necessary to improve your freedom, joy and profits. Most important, have them help you to adopt a strategic mindset. Ideally, you want a business coach with a proven, year-round coaching/accountability process.

- Accept that you alone are the agent of change. Take full responsibility for your transformation.

- After you have thoroughly read this book, start meeting with your coach on a regular basis (quarterly or monthly). In your one-on-one coaching sessions, you may wish to focus on each chapter of this guidebook.

- Buy a copy of this book for your coach and insist he or she thoroughly reads and understands its strategies. Your coach can't help you if he or she does not know the process.

- Embrace the power and benefits of repetition. Also, make good ideas your own—write them down. Take voluminous notes and capture ideas in writing.

CHAPTER 2

YOUR PATH TO GREATER FREEDOM & FORTUNE — A QUICK OVERVIEW

POINTS TO PONDER

*Don't forget until too late that the business
of life is not business, but living.*
B.C. FORBES

*If you keep doing what you've always done, you'll
keep getting what you've always got.*
PETER FRANCISCO

*It is not enough to be busy; so are the ants. The
question is: What are we busy about?*
HENRY DAVID THOREAU

Congratulations! You have admitted you are a prisoner to your business and need to break free from the tyranny of the daily grind and nauseating details. Because you are still reading, it's safe to assume that you are committed to escaping your reactive world and entering the purposeful, proactive and planning-based world of the strategic business owner. You are on your path to recovery and to greater freedom.

WHAT LEADS TO BUSINESS IMPRISONMENT?

Before we start solving our issues, we need to examine the basic causes of business owner bondage. What are the common traps? How do the chains get tighter and tighter?

Specifically, we can consider the following five to be the most common traps for business owner bondage: (1) technical tendencies (2) busyness (3) ineffective leadership and delegation, (4) inadequate or nonexistent business systems, and (5) growing business complexities.

1. **Technical Tendencies:**

    Habits determine destiny. Too many entrepreneurs are former technicians now masquerading as owners. They think of themselves as entrepreneurs, but they don't act that way. As accomplished technicians, they have a hard time letting go of such expertise and familiarity. They remain trapped in a technical comfort zone, mindset and work approach. Sadly, such technical expertise is insufficient for managing a business. Moreover, they fail to develop the visionary, strategic, and leadership skills necessary to run a successful business.

2. **Busyness:**

    Many owners confuse activity with accomplishment. They confuse busyness with results, perspiration with purpose, and efficiency (doing things right) with effectiveness (doing the right things).

Instead of working smarter, many owners hold tight to the delusion that working harder is the solution. They keep trying to shift into higher gears. The more the business grows, the harder they work and the more imprisoned they become.

No matter how much energy we expend, the wrong strategies inevitably lead to poor results—less freedom and more headaches. It is like trying to catch fish with our bare hands. No matter how many hours we work or how deep we wade, a poor strategy leads to poor results—no fish dinner!

3. Ineffective Leadership & Delegation

Far too many small business owners are, by default, small leaders. This costs them dearly. Instead of leadership, they excel at doer-ship. They are micromanagers who like to touch and control everything. They trust no one but themselves. They believe "no one does it as well as me." They seldom delegate, if at all. They mistake such busyness for business leadership. Instead of thinking and leading like owners, most think and behave like employees. Instead of reflecting and planning, they excel at sweating and doing. They act like they have a job instead of owning a business.

4. Inadequate Business Systems

The vast majority of owners don't know how to design a new business or reconstruct an existing one to be more systems-oriented and professionally equipped with processes (specific and repeatable ways to do something), procedures and policies.

Without defining and documenting the specific work that needs to be done, owners can't delegate effectively so as to eventually remove themselves from their technical roles. As a result, owners are forever feeling out of control. Tragically, most entrepreneurs have unknowingly, reactively and accidentally created an owner-centered and owner-dependent company. They are trapped!

5. **Growing Business Complexities:**

A growing business, with its increasing number of customers, transactions and problems, will eventually crush a business not properly designed and prepared to handle such growth. Without effective leadership and adequate business systems (an integrated web of processes), a growing company does not stand a chance. Growing pains are unavoidable. Producing predictable and consistent results will be nearly impossible. By failing to plan for growth, we are by default planning to fail.

These five traps lead to a life sentence of working on the chain gang—your company. Fortunately, if you are willing to change, this book can help you to escape the blues and the tyranny of technical busyness. You will no longer have to be the jack-of-all-trades for your company. Growing pains will subside. You will learn to be a master, not a servant. You will learn to lead more and work less. You will learn to shape your company by design, not by default.

THE FREEDOM & FORTUNE TRAIL FOR OWNERS

With more than 25 years of experience interacting with hundreds of entrepreneurs from a range of industries, we have learned with absolute clarity that our goal as business owners should be to design a company that is distinct from us and, quite candidly, works effectively in our absence. We should create a separate cash flow entity, not merely jobs for ourselves. It should pay us a healthy salary, plus a return on our investments of money, time and effort. We should build equity; we should build wealth. Bottom line, our roles should be to shape, manage and grow this independent and enduring asset—our business.

Our enterprise should function without us, not because of us. Yes, it sounds bizarre, but consider this: While we can be the brains behind the enterprise, we should not be like Hercules trying to hold up the entire weight of the company.

Our business should work harder so that we don't have to. We should be able to make money every day without having to work every day. The key is to invest more time and effort into our strategic leadership skills, and much less sweat into our technical skills. Our businesses should be a product of our brains, not our brawn.

We should strive to build a business that does not enslave us and does not rely on our presence every minute of every day, doing all the thinking, deciding, worrying and working. We must adopt a new way of thinking and acting.

We must become strategic business owners. Specifically, we must learn to adopt a CEO mindset; systematize and document our business; lead more and work less; create a simple business plan; utilize the leverage of marketing; effectively manage our greatest asset—our employees; and learn to let go. In short, we must transform the way we see our business and ourselves.

As strategic business owners, our primary aim should be to develop a self-managing and systems-oriented business that runs consistently, predictably, smoothly and profitably while we are not there. We should shape our business systems (again, an integrated web of processes) and employ competent and caring employees to operate those systems. We should document the work of our businesses to effectively train others to execute the work. We must make ourselves replaceable in the technical trenches of our businesses; repeat, define and document the specific work to be done, then train and delegate. This is how we begin to successfully beat the blues, escape death by details, and gain greater freedom.

With a well-documented operating system, our employees should be able to carry on the work of the business while we focus on big-picture priorities. Not only will we be able to escape the daily drudgery; we will be able to escape on an extended, work-free, guilt-free vacation knowing our company is running on virtual autopilot. We'll also have succeeded in designing and building a business that truly works and is worth a fortune. Most important, we will have gained back a personal life that is fulfilling.

To maintain freedom, independence and fulfillment as our business grows, we must cultivate effective leadership skills and operating systems. We must stop micro-managing and start leading (macro-managing). We must become more purposeful and proactive.

This guidebook will help you become a strategic business owner by addressing seven critical steps:

> **Step One:** Re-program yourself by transitioning to a new way of thinking and behaving, and by

learning new habits. Stop acting like an employee and start thinking like a CEO. Work **on** your business, not **in** your business. Adopt the theory of optimization. Be strategic, not tactical; work less, lead more!

Step Two: Systematize your company by creating, documenting and continually improving all your key processes, procedures and policies. Trust the business systems and personnel you put in place and remove yourself from the company's daily details. Be more hands-off and more brains-on. Replace yourself with other people. Define and document the work to be done. Train others and delegate the work. This operating system is your foundation for freedom.

Step Three: Increase your leadership capabilities. Excel at leadership, not doer-ship. Your business needs a clear vision and strong leader to hold others accountable, not another employee doing technical work. Help build and direct your team.

Step Four: Develop clarity of direction for your business and employees by creating a simple business plan and an effective implementation process.

Step Five: Learn to effectively manage your people, your greatest asset.

Step Six: Instead of incremental growth, engage the leverage of marketing to achieve substantial, profitable growth.

Step Seven: Learn to let go and delegate. Allow yourself to truly enjoy business ownership, your relationships and your life.

By working less **in** our business, we gain more time to work **on** our business and make those essential changes necessary to optimize our companies and our lives. This seven-step approach is the path to eliminating the blues of ownership bondage and reigniting the passion for our business and life; our formula for greater freedom, fulfillment and fortunes.

You may be skeptical, and that's normal. But ask yourself, "Are my current paths and strategies working?" If so, you wouldn't be searching for answers here. If not, we invite you to acknowledge the problems in your business, take responsibility for them, and dare to try new approaches.

SUGGESTED ACTION ITEMS:

- Review the five traps of business bondage and identify your personal challenges. Share these issues with your coach.

- Review the seven-step strategic business owner process beginning on page 38 to achieve greater freedom, financial success and happiness. Understand where the book is going and why you should commit to investing meaningful time and energy in this educational journey.

- Pledge to reconstruct your business so that you are not at the heart of every transaction, problem, decision, etc.

- Checking up on prior commitments, have you already:

▫ Selected a coach to help transform you into a Strategic Business Owner (SBO)?

▫ Committed to reading this book in 30 days?

▫ Scheduled out your regular coaching sessions?

▫ Asked your loved ones and key advisers to read this book?

▫ Taken notes, and highlighted key concepts?

CHAPTER 3

SHIFTING FROM AN EMPLOYEE MINDSET TO A CEO MINDSET

POINTS TO PONDER

If everything is important, then nothing is.
UNKNOWN

*The difficulty lays not so much in developing
new ideas as in escaping from old ones.*
JOHN MAYNARD KEYNES

*You are searching for the magic key that will unlock the door to the
source of power; and yet you have the key in your own hands, and
you may use it the moment you learn to control your thoughts.*
NAPOLEON HILL

IT'S ALL IN YOUR MIND

Through this book, we will hold up a merciless mirror that forces
you to examine cause-and-effect relationships—how your current
beliefs, strategies and actions are causing your frustrations and loss

of freedom. Please slow down, reflect deeply and adopt a new way of seeing your business and yourself as its leader. Hopefully, you will realize you must change your mindset, leadership approach and business strategies as suggested in this book to achieve a more fulfilling and financially rewarding life.

Education literally means, "to change within." Please be open to letting this book educate and change you, especially some of your assumptions and beliefs about business. All meaningful progress is the result of change. By changing your mindset and habits (repeated behavior), you change your life.

Through the years, much of our mission has centered on healing the hearts, minds and souls of beleaguered business owners. These entrepreneurs needed rescuing; not from their competition, but from their own limiting attitudes, flawed assumptions, and debilitating habits. We help owners to adjust their mindsets and convictions in order to rebuild their businesses.

Put simply, we coach entrepreneurs to conquer themselves first, the marketplace second. We help owners to evaluate and re-focus their approaches. We help them to work more **on** themselves and their businesses, and less **in** their businesses. By working less on the daily details, these owners are freed up to transform their lives and businesses for the better.

BE A CEO, NOT AN EMPLOYEE

Worth repeating; before we can fully rebuild our business, we must first adjust our mindset. We need to calm and discipline our minds to free them from reactive, counterproductive habits. We must adopt a strategic mindset and focus.

Please adopt this simple change management formula, **Have-Do-Be**. In order to **have**, we must **do**; in order to **do** effectively, we must truly **be**. For example, if you want to **have** an award-winning acting career, you must **do** certain things: take acting lessons, audition, memorize your lines, rehearse, etc. However, all this doing won't be optimally effective unless you first change your mindset—you must **be** a better actor on the inside. You cannot just play the part; you must become the part.

Similarly, in order to **have** more freedom, joy and financial success as an owner, we must **do** new strategies (i.e. systematize our business, utilize marketing, etc.). In order to optimally do these strategies, we must first **be** more effective business owners—mind, body and soul. We must change on the inside before our external realities change.

How do we escape the nauseating details and headaches of our business? How do we gain greater freedom? We must make the great mental leap from the mindset of an employee to that of a business leader. First, we must acknowledge our technical bias, our addictions to being busy, and our uneasiness with delegation. Next, we must adopt the "big picture" mindset of a CEO.

You must **be** a CEO in mind and spirit to get the results you seek. You must think, feel, see, taste, smell and hear like a CEO. This chapter will show you how.

If we don't start thinking like CEOs, it will be nearly impossible to start behaving like strategic business owners and truly working **on** our business in a proactive, purposeful manner. For many owners, jumping this wide chasm from employee to owner is tough and terrifying. However, we will never escape workaholic existences unless we stop being detailed-oriented technicians masquerading as owners.

Stop focusing on the technical work of the business; focus on the entire business. Step up and be a leader, not a micro-manager!

THE TECHNICIAN'S ADDICTION

Instead of working on their businesses, most owners are trapped working in their businesses, slaving away and grinding it out. Instead of working on tomorrow, they are preoccupied with working in today. They end up majoring in minor things. They worry about office supplies instead of office processes. They focus on accounting details instead of holding their employees accountable. They worry about the company's vision plan, instead of planning the company's vision. They react with short-term, short-lived fixes instead of proactively creating long-term solutions. They fixate on their mail, email, or phone calls instead of communicating their expectations to their key managers or employees. They obsess with doing things right, instead of doing the right things. They do the wrong type of work really well. They are chasing their tails!

Are you trapped in the body and mind of a doer instead of a leader? Be honest; do you fall into the routine of doing the work of an employee or technician instead of the work of an owner or leader? Does your focus on the mundane cause you to neglect such critical areas as vision creation, establishing priorities and goals, organizational design, business system development, profit improvement, team development, and employee accountability?

As previously discussed, you were probably a successful technician that caught the entrepreneurial bug several years ago and bought, inherited or started a business related to your technical skills. You are comfortable—too comfortable -- with handling the details. Unfortunately, the very expertise that served you so well in starting up has a strong tendency to suck you into the nooks and crannies of the business. For you, the technical day-to-day guts of the business are addictive and tough to escape. Sadly, a technician's mindset and mode of operation just aren't enough for running a business. These technical assets can be real liabilities and traps for an owner trying to be more proactive and strategic.

For example, maybe you were a gifted house painter who thought, "I should start my own painting business." From the get-go, you probably functioned in a technical capacity and never honed your leadership skills or developed the business systems. You worried about making sales and completing projects, instead of designing a painting business of which you were CEO. You dove in, got busy being busy, and started functioning as a painter, chief salesperson, estimator, bookkeeper, materials supplier, and quality control supervisor.

Consequently, you function as a jack-of-all-trades painter who also happens to own a house painting company. You are more technician than leader. Instead of focusing on the business of painting, you focus on the technical work of painting. You probably spend far too much time painting or micro-managing your other painters and not enough time painting your company's future. Because of your technical comfort zone, you are trapped doing the work of a painter, not the strategic work of a leader.

Here are a few more examples to drive home the point. Being a good computer programmer and running a successful programming business are two different roles and worlds. Writing code is technical and tactical work. Just because we know how to do the daily technical work of programming, for example, doesn't mean we know how to design, build and manage a business that does the work of programming. Programming code has not prepared us for the key functions of a business: selling, marketing, customer service, financial management, leadership, business systems, or people management. Technical experience is insufficient background for running a business.

Similarly, if our background is selling, finance or production, our bias will get us buried in the selling, financial and production details of the business. We must escape our technical conditioning, even if it means hiring others to handle such matters.

Business ownership is all about strategic leadership, not technical doer-ship. Few owners understand and appreciate such critical distinctions. Tragically, owners mistake a technician's orientation for that of an entrepreneur's. They mistake busyness for accomplishment. They confuse hard work for smart work. They have a technician's addiction to details. Sadly, they work and think like employees instead of owners. They do the wrong type of work. They fail to grasp that running a business is strategic, entrepreneurial, visionary, and requires strong leadership.

CONTRIBUTING FACTORS

If our technical background or DNA wasn't enough of a challenge, the lack of role models and faulty educations compound the problem of being addicted to technical busyness.

Let's face facts; there are too many technicians, workaholics, micro-managers and dictators in the small business world and not enough CEOs. Because of poor role models and faulty business educations, owners do not see fresh, successful alternatives.

Unfortunately, our business education system focuses too much on technical knowledge, and not enough on leadership development and organizational design. Instead of teaching an opportunity mindset, our education system focuses on everything that can go wrong. As such, we scare owners into the fatal error of thinking "I've got to do it all myself" to get it right.

As a result, owners fail to put proper systems and processes into place to help guide their employees and the business. Without systems to help them lead, owners end up micro-managing. They can't delegate effectively. Soon, their businesses outgrow their personal capabilities and time constraints. The dreaded growing pains follow because they have failed to grow their leadership skills, business systems and employees' capabilities. They are trapped on the business-owner treadmill, tackling non-strategic work, expending too much energy, and going nowhere. No wonder they have the blues! Now, the owner is at risk of burning out and the business at risk of collapsing.

PRACTICAL STRATEGIES

Wake up! You own a business, not a job. You are the owner, not another employee! Most companies are over-managed and grossly under-led. Start leading. Start thinking and planning more, and sweating less. Use more mind power, and less muscle power. Every group craves an engaged and energetic leader to direct them toward a common goal and challenge them to greater heights. Be that person for your employees. While there can be many employees, there can be only one leader. That's you, so start acting like it.

Even if you are a solo practitioner, thinking like a CEO is a critical step as you grow and replace yourself in various technical roles with new employees. Even if you decide to go it alone, you will see that the CEO mindset will pay you great dividends as you better manage your time, resources and clients/customers.

As CEOs, we need to work **on** the business: its purpose, direction, strategy, structure, systems, people, goals and account-ability processes. Again, we have to be able to see the whole business, not just its parts. We've got to have an aerial view to know where we want to go and how we want to shape our business. Instead of shuffling papers or doing the bookkeeping, we must decide how to make our company different, better, more profitable and more systems-oriented. We must think and act like business architects. Again, our goal is to design and shape a business that serves us and can work independently from us—a business that is systems-dependent, not owner-dependent. We want a business that runs nearly on autopilot and spits out cash.

As leaders, we need to be more strategically and long-term focused, and less tactical/technical, day-to-day fixated. If we don't focus on the entire business, no one else will. It will just drift or run aground. So how do we stop thinking and acting like an employee or technician? Here are nine steps to seriously consider:

1. Redefine what it means to be an owner. Regardless of your industry or the size of your business, start viewing yourself as a CEO, not an employee. Instead of seeing yourself as a player, see yourself as a head coach. The most effective owners, in our experience, prefer to view themselves as directors, conductors, facilitators or captains. Choose a powerful metaphor for being a leader that's meaningful to you.

2. To help with this mindset transformation, start referring to yourself as CEO. Put it on your business card, stationery, and website. Using the term CEO will force you to see your company as an entity above and beyond yourself, as a separate and valuable asset that needs to be professionally managed and optimized. You are not the business and the business is not you. Spend time and energy helping to build, improve and optimize this asset. For example, focus on how to grow sales, expand

your competitive advantage, and increase your value to customers.

3. Consider that as CEO, you get paid at least the equivalent of $200 an hour to professionally manage this separate entity and valuable asset—your business. Ask yourself before you touch any task, "Would a CEO do this?" Or ask, "Is this task worth me doing at a cost of $200 an hour?" Don't spend a dollar's worth of time on a dime decision or task. Elevate your vision, thinking, and tasks.

4. If you truly buy into your role as a CEO, you should be willing to give up the urgent, less important, low-value tasks you routinely handle. Realize that 80% of your results come from 20% of your talents and activities. Delegate the 80% of your activities that only produce 20% of your results. Stop doing the wrong kind of work. CEOs should think, lead and delegate—not handle trivial matters. Your job as CEO is to design and grow the business; your managers' jobs are to improve the business; and your employees' jobs are to operate the business. Here are a few more suggestions:

   □ Don't major in minor things! Don't let yourself get distracted by irrelevant, insignificant tasks and decisions.

   □ Don't let the "urgent" control your life. Put your cell phone/pager away more often. Don't be a prisoner to email.

   □ Instead of creating a to-do list, start keeping a **not-to-do** list for yourself and let go of the nonessential details. Share this not-to-do list with your team. Inform them you are excusing yourself from the daily details (usually their areas of responsibility) and are instead focusing on the big picture.

□ Use that time you've freed up to better manage your people. Guide their focus and priorities, but let them do the work.

5. Schedule time to think and plan. You must think deeply about important, strategic matters. Make time to get away from the day-to-day distractions and focus on deep thinking, planning, and decision-making. Isolate yourself to concentrate on big-picture issues. Spend time alone digesting all the information with which you are bombarded daily, and develop the big ideas to take your business to the next level of performance. Once a month, schedule a day away from the office to think and plan. With no distractions whatsoever, put on your CEO hat and spend time reviewing and improving your chief asset—your business.

6. Reserve the vast bulk of every day to tackle only your top three priorities. Selfishly guard your time and focus. Don't allow your employees to disrupt your CEO-oriented priorities and actions with countless "*Got a minute?*" interruptions; allowing such conduct creates an environment in which your time is neither valued nor respected. It also creates unproductive days, a reactive business mindset and employees who depend on you for everything. Stop these interruptions.

7. Think about CEO role models at large companies who match proven track records with solid integrity and ethics. For example, think of the former CEO at GE, Jack Welch. Read his books and understand his philosophies, mindset and strategies. Then, when you find yourself facing a challenge or difficult question, stop yourself and ask, "What would Jack Welch do?"

8. Whatever your technical expertise, consider hiring someone else to handle such technical and tactical work so you can escape the stranglehold. For example, if your background is selling or accounting, hire a competent sales or accounting manager to handle those areas. If you already have such employees on your payroll, then let them do their jobs! Get out of their zone of responsibility.

9. Finally, adopt a mindset of optimization (see the next section).

ADOPT THE MINDSET OF OPTIMIZATION

As CEOs, we need to elevate our mindsets and obsess about getting more from our current resources and efforts. We must ask ourselves and others better questions, such as, "How can our business garner greater results from every action and expenditure we make, every effort we expend, and every relationship we have?" Avoid the status quo and the complacency it breeds like a deadly virus. We must embrace fully the philosophy, "Good enough never is."

Optimization (also known as leverage) is a mindset of maximizing our results while minimizing the amount of time, effort, risk, money and energy we expend. It's all about increasing productivity, performance, profitability and payback from our ideas, assets, knowledge, systems, processes, practices, people and opportunities. Overlook nothing; leverage opportunities are everywhere. Optimization is all about utilizing your creative intelligence and limited business resources in innovative ways. In order to increase your sales, customer satisfaction, profits and quality, you must free yourself from limiting beliefs, the "We've always done it this way" attitude, and established industry practices. Your mind is an incredible force capable of discovering opportunities inside and outside your company that will lead to exponentially greater results. For example, if you follow up your direct mail campaigns with phone calls, you may multiply your sales results by staggering amounts.

Just as a tire jack can lift the tremendous weight of a car for a tire change, so too can the strategy of optimization help you significantly lift your company's revenues, improve operations, and lighten your daily load. A lever, fulcrum and slight force can lift significant weight if you know how to strategically use these tools. Learn about leverage so you can begin to elevate and optimize your business results.

To master the art of optimization, we must adopt an opportunity mindset. To leave the status quo behind, we must continually ask ourselves these kinds of questions:

- What is the most efficient use of our time, talents and treasures?

- What resources are we underutilizing?

- How can we maximize our returns/output and minimize our input?

- How can we work smarter, not harder?

- Which strategies will maximize our results?

- What processes or departments within our business are underperforming?

- What past or current relationships could we more fully leverage (i.e., customers, employees, vendors, suppliers, advisers, etc.)?

- What other industries could provide us with innovative best practices?

- Where are the hidden opportunities within our business, our employees, our suppliers/vendors, our business partners, our customer base, our competitors and our business processes?

- How can we get a greater return/payoff using the least amount of money, time, risk, etc.?

- How can we be more effective, and more productive?

- How can we get better every day in every way?

- What suggestions from our customers should we pursue first?

When we expand our minds and embrace our leadership roles, our business and opportunities will expand exponentially. The more we grow as leaders, the more our business will grow as a market leader. Think CEO, not employee. Think optimization, not status quo. Much more on leadership will be discussed in the fifth chapter, *Maximizing Your Leadership*.

Now that we understand how to think and behave like a CEO, it is time to systematize our business for smoother operations.

For your company to function at its best without relying on you, you must put robust business systems in place. These systems will give you the freedom to function as a CEO.

SUGGESTED ACTION ITEMS:

- Great transformations begin within the mind. Pledge to be open to change. Acknowledge all lasting and effective changes begin within. Believe in the BE-DO-HAVE goal-achievement formula.

- What percentage of a typical day do you spend working **in** the business, versus **on** the business? Stated another way, determine what percentage of the typical day you function as an employee instead of as a strategic business owner.

- Admit to yourself and your coach that you can no longer tolerate being an employee; you must function as a CEO. Using the term CEO will force you to see your company as an entity above and beyond yourself; as a separate and valuable asset that must be professionally handled and optimized. Consider putting CEO on your business cards, letterhead, nameplate, etc.

- Your job as CEO is to design (or re-design) and grow the business; your managers' jobs are to improve the business; and your employees' jobs are to operate the business. Again, your goal is to design and build a business that serves you and works without you—a business that is systems-dependent and not owner-dependent. You want a business that runs nearly on autopilot and spits out cash. Ensure your to-do list and your not-to-do list reflect this new reality.

- Get out of your technical comfort zone and get into your CEO zone. Admit to yourself and your coach what your comfort zone challenge will be (i.e., selling, accounting, marketing, product development, etc.). Pledge to move away from this technical bias.

- How do you stop thinking like an employee? Change your metaphors about being a business owner. For example, see yourself as the head coach, not a key player.

- To help with this mindset transformation to CEO, start viewing your company as a valuable asset separate and apart from you, one that requires professional management and care to grow it. Spend time and energy helping to build, improve and optimize this asset—the business.

- To help with this mental transformation, consider that as CEO, you get paid $200 an hour to professionally manage this separate entity and asset—your business. Ask yourself before you touch any task, "Would a CEO do this?" Or ask, "Is this task worth me doing it at a cost of $200 an hour?" Or ask, "Is this an important task or merely an urgent, yet unimportant, task?"

- Don't major in minor things! Stop doing the wrong kind of work. Don't let yourself get distracted by irrelevant, insignificant decisions and tasks. Eliminate or delegate 80% of your activities that produce only 20% of your results. Create a not-to-do list (low value, low priority, urgent tasks) for yourself as CEO and share it with your team. Inform them which activities you will no longer perform. Train others to tackle such tasks. Focus on the 20% of your talents and activities that produce the bulk of your results!

- Focus on your top three CEO priorities every day. Don't tolerate endless "*Got a minute?*" interruptions. Don't be unapproachable; rather, educate your employees on how to schedule time with you for more focused and productive meetings.

- Schedule one day each month away from the office, with no distractions whatsoever. Put on your CEO hat and spend time reviewing and improving your chief asset—your business.

- Start asking yourself, "What would the CEO at GE, IBM, McDonalds, etc. do in this situation?"

- Hire others to replace you in the technical trenches of your business.

- Adopt a mindset of optimization.

- Believe your company can get better every day in every way. Maximize your results while minimizing your company's output of time, effort, risk and money. Pledge to get greater results from every action and expenditure you make and every relationship you have.

- Repeatedly ask the optimization-type questions that appear on page 54 and 55. Photocopy such questions and keep them on your desk, in your truck, at home, etc.

- Ask all your internal and external stakeholders, "How can we improve _____ and get greater results?"

CHAPTER 4

SHAPING YOUR BUSINESS NOW TO BE SOLD LATER

POINTS TO PONDER

Organizations are perfectly designed for the results they achieve. Want new results, get a new design.
PAUL GUSTAVSON

First comes thought; then organization of that thought into ideas and plans; then transformation of those plans into reality. The beginning as you will observe, is in your imagination.
NAPOLEON HILL

Genius is the ability to reduce the complicated to the simple.
C.W. CERAM

BE A SCULPTOR TO STRIKE IT RICH

Now that we have thoroughly discussed the importance of thinking and acting like a CEO, it is time for you to become a sculptor —to mold your business to run more efficiently, effectively and consistently. Don't let your business evolve haphazardly and reactively. Proactively shape or reform it to make for smoother operations, consistent customer satisfaction and profitable results. You must turn chaos, confusion and anarchy into order and discipline. It is time to standardize and document your business.

Challenge your old beliefs about how your business should work. It is never too early or too late to shape or reform your business. It doesn't matter if your business is still on the drawing board or 20 years old; start structuring the company to run without your presence, effort and energy. You cannot control everything. You cannot control everyone. Let go! Start behaving like a strategic business owner.

You do not want to create merely a job for yourself. The ultimate goal of creating a business is to sell it one day, at the highest premium possible, whether to your employees, family members, or an outside buyer. You deserve an acceptable return on your investment of time, talent and money.

This "start with the end in mind" strategy should help you focus on building an effective business model that doesn't have you at the center of its universe, relying on your presence, personality and perspiration for its success. You should not be the business and the business should not be you. This work-in-reverse approach not only maximizes your selling price, but also minimizes your hassles and headaches while you own and run the business.

Your business model should be sculpted in such a way that it can be easily replicated dozens of times in cities around the country or world, requiring only your detailed plan, not your physical presence and exertion. Whether or not you hope to expand, such an ambition should help you focus on building a systems-dependent (not owner-dependent or people-dependent) business that generates consistent performance. You must focus on helping others get those same results. Without other people, you don't run a business—you work a job.

What is an effective business system? It is simply an integrated web of separate processes, procedures and policies. A well-designed business system allows your business to yield consistent outcomes through other people, giving you tremendous leverage and freedom. This business system will be your company's instruction manual explaining "what we do and how we do it." Some typical operating processes are as follows:

- Selling
- Marketing
- Manufacturing
- Inventory management
- Order processing/customer fulfillment
- Customer service
- Billing and accounts receivable
- Procurement/accounts payable
- Facilities management
- Accounting/finance
- Human resources (i.e. hiring, firing, reviewing, promoting, payroll, etc.)
- Information systems
- Store opening and closing procedures

A business system with these processes clearly identified and thoroughly explained will enable your employees to deliver amazing uniformity, because employee discretion is minimized. This system will also free you from having to touch every transaction, make every decision, answer every question and solve every problem. You can manage by exception. Such a carefully crafted enterprise will also give you time and space to think and act like a strategic business owner, and to enjoy those personal activities that matter most to you.

Without this business system in place, no one will pay a premium for your broken business. Why would anyone want to buy a dysfunctional business that is solely dependent on you for its day-to-day operations and survival? If it is obvious you are a prisoner to your business, no one will buy into such a life sentence. Face it; no one wants to buy a job, a series of headaches, or an owner-dependent, systems-deficient business.

To maximize your company's eventual selling price, realize that buyers want to acquire a smoothly running, money-generating machine. Buyers want to purchase a business system that runs on near autopilot, foolproof status. They want an asset that has proven processes, predictable revenue streams and strong growth potential. They want to buy a well-designed, hassle-free, cash-flowing asset, not a pain in the rear.

The more your business becomes turnkey, the greater its value to a potential buyer. If your company runs well without your constant presence, it will be worth gold to others. Until you're ready to sell, you can sit back and enjoy owning and managing a well-designed machine.

THE SYSTEM IS THE SOLUTION

During the early phase of business development or re-engineering, your brainpower and sweat equity should go into the design and creation of your business model and business systems—not into micro-managing. Spend time developing systems and performance standards early on so you can concentrate on leading later. Design an entire business template that defines and organizes the work to be done, rather than micro-managing the employees. The more you systematize your business, the less everyone will rely on you for day-to-day questions and assistance. Doing so will minimize those nagging *"Got a minute?"* interruptions, allowing you to step out of the trenches and function as CEO. Replace yourself with the system!

Plan and design the system and let your employees work it. Develop the recipe and let the employees do the cooking! Get out of the hot kitchen. Your employees should understand their roles and function within and according to the system. Once defined and documented, processes, policies and practices should be carefully followed.

With help from employees and your business advisers, identify and document all the processes, procedures and policies necessary to achieve more effective and streamlined operations. You want to get candid feedback at this stage to ensure you have an effective business model before documenting it. Start with customers' perceived needs and work backward. Re-design your business to consistently and predictably deliver the promises made to a customer during the selling process. Be sure all your back-office processes (accounting, finance, HR, technology, administration, etc.) are in alignment to effectively support the operations of the company. Design or repair any processes that are missing or faulty.

Routine work should be fully systematized and only exceptions should be dealt with on an impromptu or improvised basis. A system should eliminate arbitrary work and discretion. Your employees should have the discipline to follow the system and the freedom and authority to handle the exceptions that do not fit neatly into it. Because most potential problems and crises have been properly anticipated and converted into routine processes, "fire drills" should be greatly reduced.

Once your system is fully documented and your employees are running it, you need to let go. Trust the system, trust your team, and step away from the day-to-day workflow. With this approach, 12-hour days no longer need to be the norm. Once you allow the integrated system to run, the system itself and your employees will do the necessary work to fulfill promises made to your customers. You will not have to work as hard or as long. With effective systems, ordinary employees (properly trained) can achieve consistently extraordinary results.

The creation and implementation of this system is your solution to more freedom, fulfillment and profits. Again, plan and develop the system and let others operate it.

HOW TO SYSTEMATIZE YOUR BUSINESS

Again, your ultimate objective is to identify and document your company's key processes and practices in order to develop an operations manual/recipe for your employees to follow. In the end, you want to supply current and future employees with a detailed user's manual with job descriptions, roles, responsibilities and expectations clearly spelled out. Follow these six steps to shape your business system and develop your freedom-generating operations manual:

1. Don't rush or panic. Give yourself 4-6 months to finish your operations manual that captures (in print or electronically) every facet of your business and clearly

explains "what we do and how we do it." Oversee the process; don't do the work yourself.

2. Ensure that all processes, practices and policies are in place and functioning properly (i.e., selling, marketing, order processing/customer fulfillment, etc.). If necessary, use business advisers to ensure that your current business model has proper processes and practices in place to allow for streamlined and consistent operations. Based on this objective assessment, repair any defective processes and fill any gaps. In other words, arrange all the ingredients and walk through the steps before finalizing the recipe.

3. Once you have set the right processes in place, have your employees document like crazy. Have your current employees write down their roles, job descriptions, and daily, weekly and monthly responsibilities. If you wear multiple hats, define and document the best way to do your various roles. Then replace yourself with someone else.

4. Have departmental managers write down their departments' role, responsibilities, and daily, weekly, and monthly tasks. Also, have them document all the key processes relevant to their department (i.e., selling, operations, etc.).

5. Assign a champion to work with other managers to document your organization's company-wide (multi-department) processes that have not yet been addressed. For example, customer service most likely needs to be

tackled by several department managers as it spans multiple functional areas.

6. If necessary, hire an expert in organizational design or workflow enhancement and documentation to make the validation of your business system and creation of your operations manual a reality.

These six steps will not only document "what we do and how we do it," but also will reveal under-utilized employees, problems in your workflow, and other areas in need of improvement. Unless you know how something currently operates, you cannot begin to measure it or improve it. Without specific tasks clearly defined, it's nearly impossible to delegate. Furthermore, coach your people to think about how to improve the system. Such innovation ensures the business will continue to evolve.

I'm sure you worry that such documentation will require a great deal of work, time or money. You are absolutely right! However, you can do it right once and have a smoothly running, easy-to-manage company, or ignore this advice and forever suffer from the consequences—being overloaded, a prisoner to your business, perpetually putting out fires, answering the same old questions and handling the same old issues in a grueling, reactive, off-the-cuff manner. You can either pay the price now and regain your sanity, or continue to pay the price over the life of your ownership.

Don't get caught trying to do this all on your own. As the leader, your role is to oversee the process and creation of the master guide. Do not do it yourself! Lead the process and get expert help if necessary.

The name of the system game is documentation and continual improvement. After the initial documentation blitz, you should spend one hour a week with your team conducting workshops on process improvement. Review the documented processes, practices and policies and look for ways to repair, improve and optimize them. By continually improving your processes, your business gets better and your customers receive better service and value.

Finally, an operations manual creates additional benefits for your company:

- The company is not dependent on any one employee possessing knowledge about certain processes, policies or practices. No single employee can hold the company hostage by what he or she knows.

- If an employee is out sick or leaves, he will not take all the knowledge out the door with him.

- As you grow and add more people, your operations manual will serve as an efficient and effective training and development tool.

- Employees will not need to come to you with endless questions, problems and issues. You do not need to be the all-knowing, all-seeing oracle. They have the answer book and can seek out solutions on their own.

- Your business will not be owner-dependent, people-dependent or expert-dependent (most expensive, most experienced talent) to achieve consistent results.

- Imagine the day when potential buyers hold this operations manual in their hands and can see first-hand an overview of every key process in your company and a detailed description of "this is how we do it here." They will see a unique, proprietary business model that really works. You will see a big fat juicy check with your name on it!

- With proper business documentation in place, you will not need to hire the most experienced, most expensive managers or key employees. Because the operations of the business are captured, you can focus on hiring people who are hard working, loyal, and able to follow the game plan you have in place.

THE FRANCHISE MODEL FOR VALIDATION

Not sold on the idea of starting with the end in mind? Need more motivation to properly shape your business now to be successfully sold later? Think about this: Why do such a large percentage (some say as much as 90%) of franchise businesses survive? It's because they come with a turnkey, fully documented operations manual and proven system that works, regardless of the location and people involved. Successful franchise models are finely tuned systems-dependent businesses. They are the epitome of a strategic business.

They have identified and codified every key process (hiring people, selling, marketing, advertising, inventory management, facility layout, customer service, real estate selection and development, product fulfillment, etc.). A franchise is a business system in a box. You get a success recipe from the very start—a blueprint of a proven business model. That's why most franchise businesses succeed, so why not borrow the success strategies of this industry? It's entrepreneurship with a built-in safety net. The business owner gets an invaluable advantage—he or she has an owner's manual, an operations manual and an employee manual available from day one. Everyone, including the owner, knows her role, responsibilities and performance expectations—because they are clearly written down.

According to the Department of Commerce, more than 80% of U.S. businesses fail in the first five years. Another 80% of those survivors ultimately fail or decide to shut down in years 6 through 10. Why do 96% of business owners fail to see their 11th anniversary? It's simple—they have a technician's mindset and inadequate business systems, leadership, planning and marketing. In a nutshell, they are not strategic business owners.

By default, without a business system, companies and employees simply wing it—very little is planned and organized. There is minimal orchestration. Actions are arbitrary and random. The business depends on people instead of systems.Everyone is busy being busy, caught in a purely reactive and fatiguing 911 emergency-response cycle. Both owners and employees drain their precious energy improvising to accomplish most tasks and get burned out recreating the wheel every day.

With everyone scrambling aimlessly, no one is leading and directing—so the business just drifts. Most owners experience persistent exhaustion and blues and eventually close the doors. In our experience, most businesses don't fail because of bad concepts. Most owners simply get run down and then give up. They decide the price they have to pay is just too high.

To safeguard your company's success and your sanity, start designing or re-designing your business to be systems-oriented and self-managing. Why not borrow and adapt the success strategies of the franchise model? You do not want a business that is owner-dependent or people-dependent to achieve consistent results. You want a systems-dependent business that runs on autopilot. Life will be much easier while you are the owner and life will be much richer when you sell your business.

With a CEO mindset and an integrated business system in place, you will now have time and energy to focus on leadership, business planning, marketing, and people management.

SUGGESTED ACTION ITEMS:

- Understand and adopt the metaphor that you are a business sculptor or architect. Your job as CEO is to design and shape your business to be systems-dependent; not owner-dependent, people-dependent or expert-dependent. Sculpt a business system that works without you at the center of its very heart and soul. You must design for your freedom.

- Acknowledge the franchise model is successful mostly because it is a complete business system in a box. Pledge to borrow the success strategies of this industry.

- Fully embrace the following statements as a personal pledge: The ultimate goal of creating a business is to sell it one day, whether it's to your employees, to your family members or an outside buyer. To maximize your selling price, remember that no one wants to buy a job. They want to buy a smoothly running, effective, money-generating machine. They want to buy a successful, well-documented, organized business system that yields consistent results. Commit to yourself and your coach that you will shape your business now to be sold later.

- Have you designed your business to operate consistently and smoothly without you at the heart of every decision and transaction? If not, admit the need to re-shape your business to be more systems-dependent and less owner-dependent. Share this revelation with your coach.

- Ask your coach to hold you accountable for starting the systematization and documentation process.

- Follow the six-step process laid out earlier in this chapter to shape your business system and create your operations manual.

- If necessary, hire experts to assist with optimizing, documenting and/or continually improving your business processes.

- The name of the system game is documentation and continual improvement. After the initial documentation blitz, you should spend one hour a week with your team conducting workshops on process improvement. Review the documented processes, practices and policies and look for ways to repair, improve and optimize.

- Once you have created your operations manual, trust it and let go. This "business blueprint" should liberate you by being used to:

  □ Train and develop new hires

  □ Greatly minimize employee interruptions and questions by directing them to the operations manual

  □ Cover the gaps when employees are out sick or leave the company

  □ Save employees from having to continually reinvent the wheel, as most recurring issues, problems and crises should have been appropriately anticipated

and handled within the routine processes you created
in this operations manual

CHAPTER 5

MAXIMIZING YOUR LEADERSHIP

POINTS TO PONDER

Visualize this thing that you want. See it, feel it, believe in it. Make your mental blueprint and begin to build.
ROBERT COLLIER

The task of a leader is to get his people from where they are to where they have not been.
HENRY KISSINGER

No one can whistle a symphony. It takes an orchestra to play it.
H. E. LUCCOCK

Hopefully by now you've decided to think and act like a CEO, and you've begun the task of systematizing and documenting your business. Now you're ready to step out of the daily detail and work on the remaining strategic areas: leadership, business planning, marketing, people management and learning to let go.

This chapter will offer a crash course on leadership development. Once you have your operations manual/business recipe in writing, you will gain sufficient freedom to concentrate on growing your leadership abilities. As you expand your leadership mindset and skillsets, your business will proportionally expand. By leading more and working less, your joy will multiply and your blues will decrease.

Fight the urge to be all things to your company. If you are wearing multiple hats, you are being diverted from your chief responsibility—leadership. Increasing your leadership effectiveness will have a greater positive impact on your business than any other single factor. It will lift the shackles off the organization and free your employees' potential. Let's face it; working harder is probably not even an option for you, so why not try leading more? Again, if you don't lead, no one will.

LEADERSHIP IS EVERYTHING TO YOUR BUSINESS

If you learn nothing else from this book, fully understand and appreciate that leadership is everything to the success of an organization; whether it be a business, house of worship, political party, school, sports team, non-profit or a volunteer association, leadership is the heart and soul of an organization. Your business is no different. More important to your company's success than intelligence quotient (IQ) will be your LQ—your Leadership Quotient.

To judge the upside potential of any organization, including yours, look to its leader. The reason is simple; every organization has a leadership ceiling. An organization can rise only to the level of the chief's leadership capacity. The lower the leadership ceiling, the less room there is for everyone inside the organization to stretch and grow. Individuals cannot maximize their potential if a leader is holding them down and stunting their growth. If your people are inhibited, so is the potential of the business. Therefore, to grow your company, you must grow as a leader and grow the potential of your employees. You are only as good as your people and systems. Without question, the better the leader, the better the business.

Like most of the topics in this book, leadership is a between-the-ears kind of issue. Like any skill, it can be learned and improved upon. Become a student of leadership. To be the best leader you can be, you must study the best. If possible, observe and emulate effective leaders. If role models are scarce, read about great leaders (political, religious, educational, scientific, cause-oriented, etc.), great coaches and great business executives. Study their philosophies, mindsets, habits and strategies. Borrow from their brilliance. Adopt and adapt those lessons that seem appropriate to your situation.

Like any worthwhile skill, leadership is worth doing less than perfectly in the beginning. Allow yourself a learning curve and the chance to develop and make mistakes. To be a good leader, you must think and act like a leader.

Because thousands of books already focus exclusively on leadership, this chapter will serve to provide a mere overview of business leadership fundamentals. If you feel you need more input, you can seek additional leadership development assistance from the multitude of books, tapes, seminars, and educational and business organizations dedicated to the topic.

Are you committed to elevating and expanding your leadership quotient? Are you up to the challenge? Start by looking at business ownership as a wonderful journey of self-discovery and improvement. It is your real-world classroom for accelerated leadership development. As a more effective and caring leader, you will positively impact your bottom-line results and the lives of countless individuals inside and outside your organization.

Remember, what you become as a business owner and leader is much more important and meaningful than what you achieve or possess. Through your leadership, you will make a significant difference to others. Make becoming a better leader one of your personal quests and a higher purpose for owning your business.

LEADERSHIP 101

What does a good leader look like, sound like and do? There is not one right answer or universal model. Great leaders come in all shapes, sizes, voices and styles; however, they all share a common outcome—they oversee important achievements!

While leadership is hard to define, you know it when you see it, feel it, and hear it. An effective leader creates clarity about where the business is headed and how each team member can contribute to the cause. This clarity helps reduce confusion and wasted actions and energy. Clarity also helps your employees to make better decisions within established boundaries. As a result, you can breathe more and supervise less.

Additionally, a leader motivates individuals to work as a team and strive for a common cause or vision. A real leader pulls others along, rather than pushing them around. Leadership is about communicating, not shouting commands. You cannot coerce people to follow you for long. Command-and-control leaders seldom earn the hearts, minds and goodwill of others.

Real leadership is all about influence, the ability to make others *want* to follow you and your cause. Proof of leadership is found in the loyalty and commitment level of your followers. When you turn around, are your employees eagerly and energetically following you and your vision? If not, commit to improving as a leader.

In addition to creating clarity of purpose and direction for the organization, a leader also creates the right conditions and climate for the team to succeed. It's simple; you cannot succeed on your own. You need energized and committed followers as much as they need an effective leader. It is a mutually beneficial partnership in pursuit of a common cause. You are nothing without engaged followers. It's a symbiotic relationship—a leader needs followers to get important things done.

To help you develop a solid foundation of knowledge, consider the following fundamental leadership practices:

A LEADER CREATES CLARITY OF PURPOSE & DIRECTION BY:

- Knowing where the company is going and why
- Developing and articulating a compelling vision for the business
- Selling the benefits of this vision to employees with facts, emotions, stories, symbols, etc.
- Establishing direction, strategies and objectives for the company
- Developing a simple business plan
- Defining employees' roles and responsibilities
- Establishing clear expectations for individuals
- Developing processes to hold employees accountable for maintaining consistent results
- Encouraging individuals to work as a team; elevating the needs of the team over the needs of the individual
- Focusing employees on key priorities and results (organizational focus)

- Setting standards, monitoring performance and giving feedback

- Reminding everyone the business exists to serve and satisfy customers as well as to earn a healthy profit

- Influencing the thoughts, feelings and behavior of employees

A LEADER CREATES THE RIGHT CONDITIONS (CLIMATE, CULTURE) FOR SUCCESS BY:

- Being a true leader (CEO), not another employee; taking the time to think, plan, see the big picture and solve problems

- Building and maintaining a strong, healthy team

- Organizing resources to support the strategy of the business

- Allowing others to do their jobs, not micro-managing them

- Allowing employees to share ideas and avoiding command-and-control leadership in the decision-making process

- Helping others to believe in themselves and the mission of the company

- Serving and caring for others—being a giver, not a taker

- Getting the right people on board and the wrong people off

- Establishing a goal-oriented environment

- Maintaining open and honest communication; being open to positive feedback and constructive criticism

- Helping the company to face reality—the good, the bad and the ugly

- Accepting 100% responsibility for the results of the business

- Being bold and decisive even in the face of limited information

- Driving out fear of mistakes; encouraging experimentation and innovation

- Teaching and motivating others to reach their potential and to set higher standards for themselves

- Monitoring financial performance and taking decisive action, when necessary

- Maintaining a positive culture through interviewing, hiring, reviewing and rewarding the right type of employees

- Ensuring the company is a fun place to work

- Being a competent, caring and connected leader of good character

- Creating a sense of urgency

A company without an effective leader is like a sports team without a head coach or a game plan. Both scenarios will result in players (employees) doing their own selfish thing, running around without a purpose, with no sense of accountability, making repeated mistakes, posting lackluster performance, and most likely losing the game.

Your business doesn't need more defensive linemen; it needs an effective head coach. Let your employees do the daily "blocking and tackling." Create the game plan and let your employees play the game. Watch and coach from the sidelines, do not get in the trenches—you will lose vision of the whole field. Focus on creating clarity and conditions for success for your team.

YOU ARE 100% RESPONSIBLE

Look around your business. Whatever you like or dislike about your business and personal life, is because of you. Whatever your business has become, or failed to become, is because of you. As the business owner, whether you like it or not, you are the de facto leader. Your business is what it is, where it is, and how it is because of you, period. You are the leader. You are 100% responsible. You are the CEO, whether you are a company of one, 100 or 1,000. You are answerable for the good, the bad, and the ugly results and conditions of your business.

As such, do not blame your challenges, frustrations or problems on who is in the White House, the economy, interest rates, changing technology, globalization, industry trends, your employees or your competition. Real leaders don't hide behind excuses or try to shift the responsibility for their failures onto others. Playing that game will rob you of the opportunity that challenges provide you for meaningful self-analysis and improvement.

As leader, you are the solution to most everything that ails your company. Again, you are responsible for setting the direction and goals of the company and holding your team accountable for executing the game plan. You are responsible for shaping, systematizing and leading a business that is profitable and efficient. Unless you hire a professional business manager or president with full authority to run the business, leadership cannot be delegated. There is no such thing as effective leadership by committee or consensus. Every business needs and craves one strong leader with one clear vision. Step up!

CREATING THE VISION

Good business leaders create a vision, articulate the vision, passionately own the vision, and relentlessly drive it to completion.
JACK WELCH, *former CEO of General Electric*

Clear vision shapes and propels all impressive companies. For example, Fred Smith, founder of Federal Express, had a vision that packages could be delivered around the United States by the next morning. Walt Disney wanted to make families smile. Dominos wanted you to have hot, delicious pizza delivered to your door in 30 minutes or less, or it was free. Coke wanted to have its refreshing beverages within the reach of every person in the world. Microsoft wanted to create software that was so user-friendly and intuitive that it would make people want to have a computer on every desk at work, home and school.

Jonathan Swift said, "Vision is the art of seeing things invisible." Don't sell vision creation short. Great leaders understand, value, and appreciate the essential role of a compelling vision for a healthy and growing business. Start thinking and planning more. Escape the tyranny of the urgent, and focus instead on one of the most important tasks that only you can perform— the crafting of an exciting vision for your business's direction and destiny. Effective visions also help lead the leaders, keeping them motivated and challenged.

Be aware that your employees must buy into you as a leader before they will buy into your vision. They must believe and trust in you to believe and trust in your vision. You may need to repair relationships and establish yourself as a caring and competent leader before you can start creating and selling your vision. You will need to connect with their hearts before connecting with their heads.

Allow yourself a month for the process of creating a new vision or sharpening and updating an existing one. See yourself as the Chief Listening Officer during this early phase. You cannot build a vision or business on your own. For buy-in later, seek the input of others now. Include your employees, customers, suppliers, distributors and business advisers in the process. Spend a week or two gathering input from these stakeholders about your company's direction, strengths, weaknesses, threats and opportunities. If they do not participate in this creation phase, they will not want to participate in the vision implementation phase. Also, study your industry trends and current and emerging competitors. Do your due diligence.

After listening to and studying others, listen to your inner voice and gut. While others' input is critical, the buck stops with you. In the last analysis, you are responsible for the vision of your business, because it's what will ultimately dictate your company's direction, objectives, priorities, strategies and tactics. It is that powerful.

Find yourself a *CEO Cave* to which you can retreat, to escape the daily interruptions. This could be your home office, a coffee shop, a park, the library, or even the beach. Spend two to three days picturing what you want your business to look like in one year, three years, and five years. See things the way they can be.

Dream the big dream; unleash your spirit. See the business in your heart that you truly want to create. A bold, daring, super-sized vision, even if only partially achieved, yields greater rewards than a small, wimpy vision fully achieved.

Remember, there are no rules while you create a desired future state; however, don't deal in pure fantasy. There is a difference between a vision and a delusion. Stay somewhat grounded. You must see things the way they are now in order to visualize the way they can be. You must build from a foundation of realism, acknowledging your company's current strengths, weaknesses, opportunities and threats. Once you've gathered the facts, let 'er rip.

Grasp the future. Bring it to the present. Then, create it. Give yourself and your employees a sense of pride. Find a voice to express the common dreams, emotions, potential and needs of your team. Let your vision inspire, motivate and galvanize your team. Small visions do not stir the soul. Give people a reason to follow, something to shoot for. Make the vision intoxicating—something that captures their imagination. Show them the finish line in bright, Technicolor detail. Sell to their hearts, not their heads. People change when their feelings change, not when merely their thoughts change. Powerful visions unite groups and take them to new heights and places.

Remember, employees want purpose and passion to lift them and propel them. Find a larger purpose for your company than merely making money. Don't settle for being a random collection of people and assets trying to make a buck. A purely financial focus will not sustain the troops' morale over the long-term. Make coming to work a meaningful and fulfilling event for your employees. People want to work in a challenging and rewarding environment. They want to learn, grow and reach their potential—the full expression of their talent. People are drawn to great leaders, great visions and great causes.

Having trouble thinking big? Ask yourself bigger questions!

- Why does our enterprise exist?

- If our business were shut down, what would be missing in this world?

- What is our crusade? What could be our crusade?

- How do we engage the hearts, minds and souls of our employees?

- How can we make our company great, meaningful and different?

- How can we change our industry, community, and even the world?

- How can we measurably improve the lives of customers?

- How can we make our employees' and their families' lives better and more fulfilling?

- What higher calling or spiritual dimension can we embrace?

After listening to others' input for two weeks, and deeply reflecting for two weeks, a vision for your company should be coming into focus. Bottom line, this vision should help you and your employees reignite the fire and passion for your company's direction and purpose.

SELLING THE VISION

Once you've established a vivid image of your desired future business, you must continually and passionately share this dream with your team. After all, a vision without execution is a meaningless exercise. Become the Chief Enthusiasm Officer or Chief Storytelling Officer as you effectively sell the direction of your company.

Don't be afraid to sell emotionally. Again, you must win hearts, minds and wills. Help them feel what you feel—your passion, hope and optimism. Help them want what you want. You must transfer a picture of your vision into the hearts, minds and souls of your employees, and help them to translate the vision into real terms and achievable steps.

From this point forward, it's not only *what* you say, it's *how* you say it that matters. Be dramatic and memorable with your talks on the vision. Use a combination of facts, emotions, stories, pictures and symbols to get your point across. Don't worry; you cannot over-communicate your vision. Your employees deserve and want to know your heart's desires. Keep them informed, involved and inspired. Be a persuasive storyteller. Let employees know what you see in the future regarding your company's:

- Competitive position
- Sales and profit trends
- Market share penetration
- Number of employees
- Number of locations
- Geographic reach
- Type of customers/clients served
- Dominant niches
- Industry standing
- Product/service innovations

- Sales and marketing processes

- Structure, business systems, work flow

- Strategic alliances

- Office environment

Inspire everyone to see and strive toward this ideal business model. Such clarity eliminates confusion and wasted time and energy. Once everyone knows the vision, they will have an internal blueprint to guide their daily behaviors and decisions. It is easier for your team to grasp and move toward a clearly communicated vision than it is to inspire them via a cold, impersonal, 40-page strategic plan. Facts do not flame faith. A compelling vision (business story) will stoke the fires of faith and passion.

You aren't a charismatic leader, you say? You don't need to be! Pick a leadership style that works for you. You can be introverted and still be effective; however, you must have imagination to dream and see, taste and feel the vision. You must be an effective communicator to share this compelling future. You must be a storyteller in order to sell your concept. You must have unswerving conviction and enthusiasm for the dream. Do not be afraid to use metaphors, stories or symbols to shorten the communication path. For example, if you see your company as nimble, fast and competitive, consider using a shark or cheetah to make your point easier to understand.

While communicating the vision to others, never underestimate the influence of your actions. Put bluntly, your actions speak louder than your words. How you spend your money and allocate your time and resources says more than any speech could. Are your actions in alignment with your vision? Your employees know where your heart is by where your money and time are spent.

For example, if your vision includes having superior customer service, yet you cut corners or do not pay for your employees to be properly trained to provide that level of service, do you think they will buy into your vision? No. Put your money and attention where your vision is.

In addition to sharing your vision, you must be adroit at developing systems and an organizational structure that support this vision. In short, you must be a business architect. While the vision is the foundation of your business, you must be able to build the walls, roof, plumbing system, etc. Your marketing, selling, operations, and infrastructure must align with your vision. As we've said earlier, after you define the business, your managers should help develop the system, and your employees should run the system.

Finally, consider sharing your vision with your business advisers, investors, suppliers and customers. Be proud of your vision and let everyone know you are a dynamic, focused, energized organization. The more aligned your business is with others, the more powerful it becomes.

IT'S ALL ABOUT FOCUS

It's been said that "managers do things right and leaders do the right things." The former is about efficiency; the latter is about effectiveness. It is easy to be busy, but hard to work on the right things. Leaders must focus on doing the right things—those matters which are crucial to the success of the company. In short, effective leaders must drive the focus of the organization. Leaders must channel the time, talent, energy and resources of the organization to tackle key priorities and goals. Owners must constantly ask, "What's Important Now (WIN)?"

In today's fast-paced, technology-driven world, it's easy for people to lose track of what is most important to the enterprise. They get so caught up in the day-to-day minutia and distractions (email, voicemail, smart phones, etc.) that they must constantly re-focus and re-orient their attention to what matters. Owners need to rein in their employees' focus, too. Do not allow your employees to waste energy, time, talent and resources on trivial matters; keep them focused on the company's vision and its mission-critical priorities.

To help you manage the attention and concentration of your team, consider focusing them on six primary areas:

1. Satisfying your customers/clients

2. Getting results, not excuses

3. Improving continuously (innovation)

4. Maintaining profits

5. Keeping a long-term perspective

6. Having fun

1) Focus on satisfying your customers

Your company's primary focus should be to exceed your customers/clients' expectations. Establish a culture in which your team is motivated and committed to fulfilling your customers' needs and wants, rather than one in which they're just engaged in pushing your company's products or services. You are in business to attract, delight, and retain customers in a profitable manner—period. The real value of your business is tied directly to the future, predictable cash flow from your highly satisfied and loyal customers. Without customers, you do not have a business.

Teach your employees to value your customers, to serve them well, and to sniff out any customer problems or complaints. Keep your customers delighted and coming back for more!

As CEO, set the tone by regularly visiting the top 20% of your customers and making sure that they're more than satisfied. Find out what is on their minds, so that you can anticipate their needs. Aside from creating clarity of direction for your business, there is no better use of your time and talents.

2) Focus on getting results

Next, focus your team on achieving results for your company. Establish a climate in which activity is not confused with accomplishment—a place where thinking and planning are admired, and actual results are valued more than busyness. Reward effectiveness (doing the right things) more highly than simple efficiency (doing things right). Insist on intelligent, meaningful action and discourage procrastination (paralysis-by-analysis) and excuses. As a leader, one of the most important jobs you have is to establish a goal-oriented environment with a solid expectation of performance. Insist on results; do not tolerate excuses.

The chapter on business planning and implementation will cover how to set and achieve business goals.

3) Focus on continual improvement

After satisfying customers and insisting on results, the next focus area should be on continuous improvement. If your company is not improving, it is declining. Every day your company sits idle is one more day for the competition to gain strength and overtake you. Therefore, establish a climate in which continuous improvement and innovation thrive. Do not let your employees fear failure or making mistakes; just work towards eliminating repeated mistakes. Failure is not fatal, but failing to change might be.

As CEO, you must drive out fear from your organization. If your company is not failing occasionally, either your goals are too low or your rate of innovation is too slow. Your employees should be encouraged by your example to adopt the attitude that failure is not painful or shameful. Failure is merely valuable feedback on what not to do next time. Failure is fertilizer for future success. Failure is an incredible gift if properly viewed and used. If we are moving closer to our goals, we are winning. The quicker we fail and modify our approach, the quicker we reach our goal.

Motivate your employees to continually improve what they do and how they do it. Help them to think critically about how to improve their roles, responsibilities and contributions to the cause. Incentivize them to constantly be looking for ways improve your systems and processes. Remind them, "Good enough never is." Refer back to the theory of optimization for powerful questions to ask yourself and your team.

Encourage employees to try new things. Experiment, experiment, experiment! Take small steps to test ideas and learn more in the process. If something works better, keep it. If it doesn't, lose it. Know when to cut your losses. Admit mistakes and let go of failed ideas fast; fail fast, fail cheap. Keep your ego in check.

Once a week, facilitate a one-hour business improvement workshop. Release the brainpower of your organization. Assign every good idea that surfaces a champion and a due date, and outline the key action steps to take toward its implementation. Good ideas not put into action are worthless. Reward employees for successfully applying ideas that increase revenues, cut costs, improve operations or morale, or improve customer satisfaction.

Also, encourage healthy debate amongst your team. Allow everyone, in a constructive manner, to challenge ideas, policies and strategies. Even allow for productive and constructive conflict. When ideas are put to the test, they improve.

4) Focus on profits

Next, concentrate on growing your revenues and, most importantly, your profits. Aim for both top-line and bottom-line growth. Focusing only on revenue growth is ego-driven and not smart. Cash flow and profits are your lifeblood. Keep your gross margins strong.

Also, while cost containment is important to the health of your company, do not over-emphasize slashing costs. Stay on the offensive, not the defensive. Revenue growth is nearly endless, cost cutting is limited—you can only cut so much before you do real damage. Some costs are really strategic investments in the future of your business (i.e., new equipment, advertising, training, and development, etc.).

Do yourself a favor. Hire the best CPA you can afford—one who not only understands numbers well, but is also conversant with topics covered in this book. An entrepreneurially-minded CPA who understands the needs of a growing business and owner is an invaluable asset and worth the premium.

5) Focus on the long-term

Remember, you are in business for the long haul. Do not be short-term oriented. Business is a marathon, not a sprint. Do what is right, always. Maintain the highest integrity and ethics, because your reputation is everything. Business is about sustaining lifelong relationships with customers, employees, investors, suppliers, advisers, etc. Repeat business is absolutely critical to the very life force of your company. Do not take shortcuts.

To help drive home this concept, consider the lifetime value of your customers. Over the average service life (number of years) of a customer, how much profit does your typical customer provide you? For example, if a typical company buys from you several times a year, yielding you a total annual profit of $1,000, and you generally retain such a customer for 5 years, the lifetime value for a typical customer is $5,000. Stated another way, every time you attract a new customer and serve them well, odds are that customer will be worth $5,000 to your business over time.

Once you're aware of this value, you and your employees are more likely to think twice about upsetting or losing a customer. This lifetime value calculation also validates the idea that you should spend money (acquisition cost) to attract new customers. As long as you break even on acquiring a customer and know with certainty that there is considerable back-end or repeat business, it makes sense to spend money on marketing and selling. Invest a little to make a lot; that's leverage.

6) Focus on having fun

Lastly, focus on making business fun. Celebrate worthwhile progress toward your goals. Celebrate your company's successes often and reward your employees for superior performance. Come up with excuses to praise your team and recognize accomplishments Share the joy. Make coming to work a meaningful and fulfilling event. In fact, appoint a CFO (Chief Fun Officer) to think of clever ideas and organize activities, based on employee feedback, to energize the work environment with excitement and positive vibes.

As much as they value their paychecks, good employees also want to learn and grow, to be challenged and rewarded, and to fulfill their needs to be social beings. Make your culture an enjoyable place to work.

DON'T MICRO-MANAGE

Real leadership is rare; micro-management is too common. Stop trying to play every darn instrument yourself and start conducting the orchestra. If you don't, who will?

As a strategic business owner, your primary aim should be to develop a self-managing and systems-oriented business that can run consistently, predictably, smoothly, and profitably without you. Shape and own the business system, and hire competent, caring employees to operate the system. As we've noted earlier, you need to clearly document the work of your business so you can effectively train others to execute the work—then stand back and let them do it. Don't suffocate the talents and growth of your employees.

Don't be a super-worker, be a supervisor! Snuff the "I'll do it myself" and "No one does it as well as I do" attitudes. Learn to delegate. Engage your coach to help you with this critical skill.

If someone else can do something 80-90% as well as you, give it up! Do not spend a dollar's worth of time on a dime task. Know your areas of brilliance, and delegate most everything else. Do those things that only you can do as CEO and assign the rest to others. You need to free up time for the kinds of CEO-specific activities that will make your vision a reality. That said, be sure to delegate, not abdicate or dump. Stay in touch with those to whom those tasks have been allocated, and monitor their progress.

Adopt the attitude that your time is valuable, and learn to discriminate between various activities. Before doing a task, ask, "Does this task directly increase profits, significantly reduce costs, improve customer satisfaction, or help to build a better business?" If it doesn't, dismiss the task or delegate it. If the task is not worth $200 an hour, find someone else internally or externally to do it at a cheaper rate. You must realize that your CEO thoughts and actions (building systems, leading, planning, holding people accountable, coaching other leaders, etc.) are worth at least $200 per hour. If not, you will never learn to be effective at delegation.

You cannot delegate non-specifics, so be sure that the tasks are well defined, then get out your managers' and workers' way. Don't meddle; monitor. Instead of doing their jobs for them, help clarify their roles, responsibilities, goals and tasks, and simply hold them accountable for getting things done. Coach more and play less in the game.

Once they demonstrate competency and character, give your employees the authority to make things happen. Let them do their jobs. Let them tackle projects on their own and come to you only when they need further guidance. Instead of micro-managing the process, manage by results. If you set up your systems correctly and train properly, you will be able to manage by numbers and on an exceptions-only basis.

The operative assumption here is that you are paying your employees and managers good money to do their jobs. If you aren't paying adequate wages, beware! If you pay peanuts, then expect to attract monkeys.

Leadership is less about doing, more about thinking, planning and overseeing what others do. You are in business to create jobs, not work a job.

BE BOLD, BE DECISIVE

Followers want their leaders to be bold, focused and decisive. It's up to you to make things happen. Do not get caught in the "ready, aim, aim, aim" loop. When you've done your strategic planning and analysis, have the guts to pull the trigger. Here are some suggestions:

- Generally, inaction is more costly than action. Implementing a good idea today is usually a better strategy than waiting indefinitely for a great idea to come down the pike. Most times, value movement over meditation, and action over analysis.

- Even with limited information, continue to make decisions. Don't delay.

- Know where you are going and why.

- Listen to and trust your inner voice and instincts.

- Go for growth over status quo. Don't settle for the ordinary.

- Go for breakthroughs, not incremental changes.

- Write your own rules.

- Zealously focus on important goals and favor action.

- Have a good plan and great execution.

KEEPER OF REALITY

As a leader, you are the keeper of reality and the seer of truth. One of your primary tasks is to help define reality; to remove the blinders, to expose blind spots and to reveal delusions.

Be neither a gushing optimist nor a panicked pessimist. Be a realist with undying faith in the potential and promise of your company. Know your company and your team's strengths, weaknesses, opportunities and threats. See your ever-changing situation for what it really is, not what it was or what you or others wish it to be. Do not allow fallacies or blind spots to take your company down. Burn off the fog that is clouding your objective view. Armed with the facts and a strong dose of reality, you can always make necessary adjustments. Deal in fact, not fiction.

SHARE THE KNOWLEDGE

Learn to share existing knowledge within your company and seek fresh ideas and strategies from the outside. Knowledge is power, but only if it is applied. The cumulative knowledge in your organization is immense; however, most businesses do not openly share knowledge, best practices, or mistakes.

If you do not proactively encourage sharing, your employees will tend to hoard knowledge and hide mistakes, either in an attempt to jockey for power or simply to avoid embarrassment. You must encourage an atmosphere in which all knowledge, good and bad, is to be shared. The most innovative ideas can come from those people you'd least expect to hear from. Be committed to finding the best way, not in having your own way. Tap into everyone's brainpower.

As CEO, continually ask your employees:

- "If you were CEO for a day, what would you change and why?"

- "Give me three changes we could make that would substantially grow our profits."

- "Describe three ways that we could dramatically improve our operations/customer fulfillment."

- "Give me three ways to significantly improve our customer satisfaction rates."

- "What are three actions you'd take to raise office morale and improve our team spirit?"

At all costs, you must avoid mental constipation. Learning is leverage. As CEO, you need to meet with and learn from other entrepreneurial CEOs. Join CEO Roundtables via your Chamber of Commerce, the Young Entrepreneurs Organization (YEO), the Young Presidents Organization (YPO), or start your own CEO Mastermind Group. Find a mentor who has successfully mastered the company-building process and effective leadership. Again, use your coach to hold you accountable for learning, sharing and innovating.

Don't become myopic. Look beyond your industry for ideas. Consider how other industries are marketing, selling, operating and working. Read trade magazines from different industries. Carry a notebook or mini-recorder to record those fresh ideas. As you expand your mind, you're expanding your options, possibilities, strategies and your business.

Gather outside directors who can bring diversity, expertise, objectivity and experiences to your business. Add people who can raise issues, challenge you, and make suggestions. Consider dismissing those who can't.

Finally, hire top-notch advisors (i.e., CPA, banker, attorney, executive coach, specific consultants, etc.) and fire those who do not bring real value. Hire ones that specialize in working with fast-growing, entrepreneurial companies. Make sure they understand the concept of working "on," not "in" a business, as well as the importance of leadership, business systems, planning, marketing, and people management. They will more than pay for themselves.

FINANCIAL STEWARDSHIP

Make sure you've got a handle on the numbers, and that you know the financial health and trends of your organization. Learn to read income statements, balance sheets and cash flow statements and to understand what they are telling you. Don't try to manage your business by gut instinct; the numbers never lie. Constantly look for innovative ways to grow revenues and reduce costs.

Learn to monitor your company's vital signs. Have your accounting manager or CPA create "dashboard metrics" to help you steer your business. These are simple, key measures that let you see the performance of your business at a glance. Depending on your company and industry, these metrics could include daily/weekly sales, weekly cash flow, backlog report, on-time shipments, returned items, gross profit margins, line of credit balance, production numbers, accounts over 60 days, etc.

Do yourself a tremendous favor: Hire a terrific chief financial officer or controller to manage your accounting and financial matters. Make sure this person knows how to gather, interpret and explain financial data in simple terms. Be sure that he or she is proactive in her advice to you and focused on the future, not just past performance. Your advisory team should include a top-notch CPA, a banker, an insurance professional and a financial planner. Sharp advisers who understand the issues a business owner faces are worth their weight in gold. Do not cut corners here. Hire the best and their value and benefit will far exceed their cost.

SUGGESTED ACTION ITEMS:

- Leadership means everything to the success of your business and personal life. True leaders create clarity of direction, priorities and expectations. To grow your business, freedom, and fulfillment, you must grow your leadership capacity.

- Rate your leadership effectiveness on a scale of 1-10, and be honest. Pinpoint those leadership areas in which you need to improve. Share these evaluations with your coach and other key advisers. Have them hold you accountable for growing as a leader.

- Buy books, DVDs or CDs on three great leaders you admire (i.e., CEOs, coaches or political/religious/cause-oriented leaders). Model their philosophies, mindsets and strategies.

- Admit to yourself and your coach that you are 100% responsible for the results and condition of your business. No more excuses!

- Schedule a month in which to tackle vision creation for your business. For the first two weeks, act like a Chief Listening Officer. Get input from all your internal and external stakeholders (i.e., employees, customers, CPA, banker, attorney, consultants, suppliers, vendors, and investors). Ask them to share their thoughts about your company's SWOTs (strengths, weaknesses, opportunities and threats).

- After listening to what others have said, it's time to listen to your heart and your gut. Spend a few days in your *CEO Cave* digesting the input from others, along with industry trends, competitive positions, and your thoughts on your company's SWOTs. Launch your vision from a platform of reality; however, create a powerful vision (crusade) that engages the hearts, souls, minds, bodies and imaginations of your employees.

- Once you create your vision for the company, start "selling" the vision to all your internal and external stakeholders. You are now the Chief Enthusiasm Officer or Chief Storytelling Officer. Share the vivid and exciting details of how the business will look in one, three and five years.

- If you are not an effective storyteller, have your coach or another adviser work with you. While you don't need to be a dynamic or charismatic leader, you need to be able to sell your vision effectively (tell the business story). Take a public speaking course if you need to. Also, be aware that your actions and where you spend your time and resources send a stronger message than your words. Both your words and actions need to be in alignment with your vision.

- You must drive the focus in your company on What's Important Now (WIN). Make sure your team is doing the right things, not merely doing things right. With the help of your coach and key managers, focus your team on six primary areas:

  □ Exceeding the expectations of your customers: You are in business to attract, serve, delight and retain customers in a profitable manner.

  □ Valuing results, not tolerating excuses: Establish a goal-oriented culture with solid expectations of intelligent action and meaningful results.

- □ Continuous improvement: "Good enough never is." Drive out fear and enable your employees to experiment like crazy on new ideas, concepts and approaches. Test new ideas and keep the ones that work better than existing approaches. Conduct weekly one-hour business improvement workshops. For every good idea worth pursuing, assign a champion, due date and key steps. Monitor progress and insist on aggressive implementation and follow-through.

- □ Achieving profitable growth: Focus on both revenues and profits. Cut costs and grow profitable revenues. Engage the best CPA you can afford.

- □ Maintaining a long-term perspective: Do not take shortcuts, and always do what is right. Repeat business is the life force of your company. Know the lifetime value of your customers.

- □ Having fun—Celebrate often, praise often, have fun.

- Be bold and decisive. Practice making decisions (based on the known facts) quickly, and change your mind slowly, if at all.

- Learn to delegate. Learn to trust your people and systems. If a task isn't your area of brilliance, delegate. If someone else can do the task 80% as well as you can, hand it over to him. If the task is not worth $200 an hour, find someone else internally or externally to do it for less.

- Ask your coach to help you with delegation.

- Face reality. See your company without any delusions or blind spots. See the way things really are, not what they were or what you want them to be. Always have a fix on your company's SWOTs.

- Learn to share knowledge and seek fresh ideas:

  □ Tap into everyone's brainpower. Ask internal and external contacts to pretend to be CEO of your company for a day and give ideas to improve profits, sales, operations, products/services, customer satisfaction, team spirit, etc.

  □ Join a CEO peer group to exchange ideas, challenges, solutions and fresh approaches. Look beyond your industry for ideas and solutions.

  □ If you haven't done so, form a board of outside advisers that will share their diversity, experiences, objectivity and ideas with you.

- Get a handle on your company's financial numbers. Learn about basic accounting concepts and financial reports. Have your CPA create simple "dashboard metrics."

- Hire a proactive and top-notch chief financial officer, controller or accounting manager who can gather, interpret and explain financial results and trends. Hire the best CPA you can afford.

CHAPTER 6

CLARITY OF DIRECTION: A SIMPLE BUSINESS PLAN

POINTS TO PONDER

A good plan is like a road map: it shows the final destination and usually marks the best way to get there.
H. STANLEY JUDD

The best plans are straightforward documents that spell out the who, what, where, why and how much.
PAULA NELSON

Our goals can only be reached through a vehicle of a plan, in which we must fervently believe, and upon which we must vigorously act. There is no other route to success.
STEPHEN A. BRENNEN

KEEP BUSINESS SIMPLE

To be an effective CEO, you must adopt a big-picture perspective. As leader, don't over-complicate business. Keep it simple and straightforward. Simplicity allows for clarity of focus, and focus allows for superior performance.

As owner or CEO, you are solely responsible for the company's leadership process—its direction, strategy, focus, goals and accountability, **and** the business development process—building a systems-based business that is self-managing, self-improving, and nearly runs itself. Toward that end, there are five processes you'll want to be sure are well documented and running smoothly; marketing, selling, operations (customer fulfillment), customer service and back-office functions.

Let's address the first four: In the simplest terms, the marketing process generates leads, the selling process generates customers by closing leads, and the operations process fulfills the promises made to the customer. Completing the business cycle is the customer service process that follows up with the customer to ensure satisfaction with the current transaction and to uncover any unmet needs.

Because the purpose of any business is to find, satisfy and keep customers, these processes should be your top priorities and areas of focus. Your back-office functions, while important, exist to support these primary objectives. These back-office support functions are: a finance/accounting process to manage money; human resources to manage employee issues; and an infrastructure to manage technology, facilities, administration, etc.

Spend your time and energy focusing on your company's core processes and competencies—those functions that your organization does extremely well, and which add real value to the customer. Keeping business simple will help you stay focused on what is most important.

To simplify your business and your life even more, consider outsourcing your back-office functions, such as payroll processing, tax preparation, legal, HR, technology, and facilities management. Seek advice from your CPA, attorney or banker about outsourcing arrangements.

PLANNING FOR RESULTS

How do you create a simple business plan? How do you achieve results? Again, you must keep things simple and focused. With your team's involvement, agree on and set annual goals. Then, on a 90-day cycle, gather your team and hold your people accountable for the agreed-upon results. This implementation process is just as important as the goals. Do not tolerate excuses; insist on execution and results.

Select a few key strategies and implement like mad. Success is more about execution than anything else. Focus on the vital few instead of the trivial many. Energy focused on a few highly important goals is powerful.

Please note, we are not talking about setting goals to achieve incremental improvements in performance or processes. We are talking about big and bold goals—goals on steroids. Be innovative and think big. Go for breakthroughs, not merely incremental gains. Realize there are no rules or restrictions. As long as what you do is moral, legal, and ethical, do not be shackled by company history or industry standards or practices. Lose the "we have always done it this way" mentality, and shake things up.

At a minimum, performance goals should be set in the critical success areas we just discussed: leadership, business systemization, marketing, selling, operations (fulfillment), customer service and back-office operations. In fact, your annual business plan could be as simple as three to five monster-size goals in each one of these key areas. Once you have your annual goals established, assign a person to champion each cause. Give each person the authority, time and tools to make things happen. On a 90-day cycle, hold each person accountable for progress on his or her goal(s).

These audacious, challenging and adrenalin-inducing goals should be SMART (Specific, Measurable, Achievable, Really Desired and Timed). Force your people to stretch. What gets measured gets done. What gets rewarded gets repeated. As a leader, insist on aggressive implementation, follow-up, follow-through and results. Intentions and plans are mostly meaningless; implementation is where success is found.

HIRE A RETREAT FACILITATOR

Consider the potential benefits of having an annual off-site strategic retreat with your management team and/or key players. We strongly encourage hiring an objective facilitator to ensure there is honest dialogue and full participation, and that all key barriers and issues are addressed. Buy-in must be achieved, and a workable action plan must emerge. By the time the retreat wraps up, every participant should know the answers to the following questions:

- Where are we going (clarity of direction)?
- What's expected of me (my contribution)?
- How will I be measured (accountability)?
- How will I benefit (rewards)?

Before the retreat, this facilitator should interview each of your managers and/or key employees on a one-to-one basis to get an honest lay of the land. Typically, the facilitator will seek critical feedback and input by asking questions like these:

- Please share your thoughts about your company's...
  - Strengths
  - Weaknesses/Areas to improve
  - Opportunities
  - Threats
  - Competitive landscape
  - What makes you unique, different, valuable
- Describe your management team's...

  - Strengths/Weaknesses/Opportunities/Threats
  - Ability to handle growth
  - Ability to lead
  - Ability to delegate
- Please share with me thoughts about your personal...

  - Strengths/Weaknesses
  - Role/responsibilities
  - Ability to lead
  - Ability to delegate
  - Expectations for the strategic retreat
- If you were made CEO...

  - What changes would you make?
  - How would you dramatically improve our revenues?

- □ How would you dramatically improve our operations?

- □ How would you dramatically improve our value to customers?

- □ What people would you dismiss?

- □ What people would you cultivate to lead?

- On a scale of 1-10, how would you rate the company's performance in each of these areas:

  - □ Sales

  - □ Marketing

  - □ Operations (customer fulfillment)

  - □ Leadership (clarity of vision, direction, objectives, accountability)

  - □ Business processes

  - □ Customer service

  - □ Back-office functions (accounting, finance, HR, technology, etc.)

  - □ Our people

- On a scale of 1-10, how clear is the company's current...

  - □ Vision/Direction/Focus

  - □ Goals

  - □ Strategies

  - □ Accountability process

  - □ Review and compensation process

- On a scale of 1-10, how clear is/are your...

- Role(s)
- Contributions
- Responsibilities

Armed with these diagnostic insights, your facilitator should be able to lead a productive retreat that improves the performance of your people and company.

Also, strongly consider hiring the facilitator or a coach to come back on a monthly basis to ensure that the business plan is being properly implemented. This person can help hold your company and team accountable for taking action.

SUGGESTED ACTION ITEMS:

- Keep business simple.
- Set annual and 90-day goals in the critical success areas: leadership, business systems, marketing, sales, operations (customer fulfillment), customer service, and back-office functions.
- Conduct an annual strategic retreat at an off-site facility.
- Strongly consider hiring a facilitator to do pre-interviews, orchestrate the retreat, and help with post-retreat implementation.

CHAPTER 7

PEOPLE MANAGEMENT

POINTS TO PONDER

*Coming together is a beginning; keeping together
is progress; working together is success.*
HENRY FORD

*It doesn't make much difference how much other knowledge
or experience an executive possesses; if he is unable to achieve
results through people, he is worthless as an executive.*
J. PAUL GETTY

*There is no such thing as a self-made man. You will
reach your goals only with the help of others.*
GEORGE SHINN

We've covered many topics relevant to the skills of people management in the previous chapters on leadership and business planning, including:

- Leadership basics
- Being 100% responsible as the owner
- Creating and articulating a vision

- Focusing your team on customers, results, innovation, profits, establishing a long-term horizon. and having fun
- Avoiding micro-management
- Delegating
- Being bold and decisive
- Facing reality
- Sharing knowledge
- Keeping business simple
- Creating a simple business plan
- Setting and achieving 90-day goals

In this chapter, we will focus on the critical importance of getting the right people on board; how to keep them accountable; how to establish trust with your team; and how everything you do contributes to the culture of your company.

YOUR GREATEST ASSET

You cannot reach your vision and goals without the help of others. Your greatest asset is people—the "right" people—who share your company's values, ethics, personality, culture and vision. Your primary objective is to get the right people on board, and keep them going in the correct direction. Recruiting, training/ coaching, developing and retaining your competent employees are critical success factors for your company and among your top responsibilities as a leader. Your focus should be to develop others and create the conditions in which they can succeed; to unleash the full human potential of your organization.

WHAT EMPLOYEES WANT

Here is an unscientific crash course in what employees want:

- To know where the company is headed and why
- To know their roles, responsibilities and what is expected of them
- To know how they will be evaluated and rewarded
- To utilize their talents in the best way possible
- To feel appreciated and valued—that their work and ideas matter
- To be coached—challenged, motivated and held accountable
- To have the necessary tools, training and authority to do their jobs well
- To contribute in a meaningful way to the company and its mission
- To grow, develop and reach their potential
- To have an emotionally connected, competent leader support their success

HIRING/FIRING BASICS

Hire for talent, not just résumé data. Be sure to hire emotionally engaged people, people with passion in their eyes and fire in their gut. Match their talent to their position—again, help them to be successful. Don't hesitate to use personal assessment tests to better understand the aptitudes, attitudes and talents of potential employees.

While you should hire people slowly, fire them quickly if they do not fit your culture and can't operate within your system. Do not let emotionally disengaged people or negative people infect your company. Don't waste time and energy trying to rehabilitate poor performers (the lower 20% that cause 80% of your headaches). Spend your time and effort with your top performers, the top 20%. This top 20% will produce 80% of your company's results. For your business to grow, you must find and develop that top 20%.

Because you cannot control everything, the development of your system and your people are paramount. Hire excellent leaders and managers, then let your managers hire competent employees (not necessarily brilliant ones) to work the system; hard working and loyal people who will follow the system and execute their duties according to documented practices. Again, hire emotionally engaged people with passion in their souls. Their focus should be on working the system and improving the operations manual, as necessary. They should not be free-lancing, improvising or winging it.

DEVELOPING YOUR PEOPLE

True leaders care about their people and their on-the-job education and development. Make sure you have a fair annual performance review process in place. Employees crave helpful feedback on how they are performing. When it comes to your employees, view yourself as an educator and developer of people. Make sure they know your system, as well as your expectations for their roles and responsibilities within it. Continually share your vision and your guiding principles with them, because clarity of purpose is critical to employees. Give them a defined structure, order, sense of purpose and meaning. If you take care of the team, the team will take care of your business.

Also, make certain your employees understand bottom-line fundamentals and how they can contribute to improved profits. They need to know how their daily thoughts, actions and inactions impact profits and customer satisfaction. Let them feel a real sense of responsibility for profits and clients. Make it clear that you expect them to look out for new ways to grow revenues, eliminate inefficiencies and improve business practices. Most employees will try to live up to your expectations.

As leader, you should be developing future leaders in your organization. You gain tremendous leverage by developing the leadership skills of your people. This leadership development effort also helps with crisis management events, succession planning, and eventually selling the business. Focus more time, energy and effort on taking care of your best performers, and much less time on your more problematic employees. The more leaders you develop, the greater impact they will have throughout the organization. To stop working in your business, you need to be able to hand over the reins of day-to-day operations to competent leaders.

You can also leverage past employees. Keep track of where your prior employees have gone. They are your alumni. If they left on good terms, keep in touch and maintain some form of ongoing communication. They can refer you potential employees, customers and may even rejoin your organization.

KEEP YOUR PEOPLE ACCOUNTABLE

Too many leaders do not hold their people accountable for reaching established goals or performance standards. Such lack of accountability is one of the deadliest business mistakes.

What's currently happening in most small businesses? Meetings are held, issues are discussed, solutions are proposed, and goals are set. Unfortunately, the story usually ends there. Implementation is weak at best. Follow-up and follow-through are missing. Accountability is missing too, so ideas, strategies and tactics never get off the ground, and promises fall through the cracks. What a waste of time and talent!

Why does this happen? Owners are not functioning as leaders. They are not monitoring progress on goals. They are too deeply engaged in the details of the business to focus on the performance of others or the overall performance of the company.

Moreover, too many business owners try to be liked instead of respected. Holding people accountable can be confrontational at times. Many owners avoid tension, conflict and ongoing performance reviews. Such avoidance is dangerous to your business and the development of your people. Don't be everyone's buddy. Don't try to be popular. This isn't high school. As a leader, you need to be respected, not necessarily liked. Above all, you are their boss and a challenging coach that demands the best of each player.

Meet with your key employees or managers at least once a month for a one-on-one accountability session. Remind them of your expectations. Help them to grow and improve. Again, when you create clarity of expectations and standards, there is less confusion and more effective delegation and accountability.

Be very careful about letting your employees become your social friends. You need to remain objective to make decisions in the best interest of the company. If you want a friend, get a pet. If you want to be liked by everyone, sell your business and get a job. Trying to please or be liked by everyone is a sure path to disaster.

Give people the responsibility, freedom, resources and support required to get important things done. Let them know they will be held accountable for getting results. Continually remind them of your expectations. Monitor their progress and intervene only when necessary. Give them meaningful feedback. Praise an employee's progress on goals in public and criticize their poor performance in private. Feel free to express your disappointment and frustration to your entire team, but save the harsh criticism for an individual for behind closed doors. Praise in public; criticize in private.

Here are some basic ground rules for effective accountability:

- Never let committees, groups or multiple people be accountable for making things happen.

- Make sure one person/one champion is responsible and accountable for each key assignment.

- Establish goals and clarify due dates for results.

- Conduct regularly scheduled follow-up meetings to gauge progress on goals and hold people accountable.

- If your employees consistently fail to get important things done, give them different jobs or replace them with new people.

Do not allow poor implementation to infect your business; we all know where unmet good intentions can lead. You have only two choices—establish a culture that tolerates excuses or one that insists on performance. Do you want more excuses or execution of goals? Accountability is the key to improvement, and you're responsible for providing it for your employees.

People want to be held accountable and challenged. They also want constant feedback on their performance. They want to learn and to grow. They even desire a healthy environment of discipline. All this helps them develop and reach their potential. Accountability is beneficial feedback that shows you care. Make certain your employees feel appreciated and important—they crave it!

As CEO, who will hold you accountable? Again, get a coach or enlist a board of advisers. Such people will help you reach your greatest potential.

TRUST OR BUST

Trust is the fabric that holds a company together. If people do not trust you, they will not trust your vision or strategies. If you lose your character and reputation, you will have lost everything. Here are some suggestions:

- Do what you say you will do. Keep your promises.

- In good times and in bad, be ethical, moral, and trustworthy. Your personal integrity must be above reproach.

- Your words and actions must be in alignment. Walk the talk. Be a straight shooter.

- Honesty is paramount.

- You must lead by example.

- Be an authentic person—what people see is who you are.

- You must share the good, the bad and the neutral news with your team. Open communication is a must.

- No employee will complain about being kept too informed, too involved or too inspired.

- Be sincere and always speak from the heart—phonies are easy to spot.

- Build trust with deep listening.

Trust must be earned over time; however, it can be lost in an instant and is very difficult, if not impossible, to rebuild. Know that any untrustworthy behavior will cost you good employees. Good employees do not leave bad companies; they leave bad leaders.

CULTURE CREATION

As leader, know that you set the tone, pace, environment and personality of your company. By your consistent actions, you establish what the company values and what gets rewarded. You lead by example and, to a large extent, shape the culture of your organization.

In large part, you maintain the culture by participating in the interviewing, hiring, reviewing and rewarding of your employees. Always make time for these critical activities.

Above all, try to create a culture where your people feel appreciated and important, and where they can fully use their talents and reach their potential. William James said that, "The deepest principle in human nature is the craving to be appreciated." If you achieve such a supportive and fear-free culture, you will have created a successful company with solid retention of your employees.

Make coming to work enjoyable. Identify, celebrate and remember your company's victories. Capture them in stories that you repeat, especially to new hires.

SUGGESTED ACTION ITEMS:

- Your greatest asset is finding, hiring, developing and retaining the "right" people for your company. Get the right people on board, the wrong people off, and the ship heading in the right direction.

- Concentrate on your best performers, not your worst. Spend time developing future leaders—you will gain tremendous leverage.

- Leverage past employees. Keep in touch with your alumni. They can feed you new customers and new employees.

- Hold your people accountable. Do not try to be everyone's buddy. Insist on results. Conduct an annual or bi-annual performance review to evaluate the contribution of every team member.

- Implement an ongoing accountability process for your key goals. Conduct weekly accountability sessions to gauge progress on goals. Insist on performance and results; do not tolerate excuses.

- Trust is everything. If your employees don't trust you, they will not follow you. Keep your promises. Walk the talk. Share good news, bad news and neutral news. Trust your employees and they will trust you.

- You set the tone, pace and climate of your business. Create a culture where your employees feel appreciated, important and capable of reaching their full potential.

CHAPTER 8

MASTERING THE POWER OF MARKETING

POINTS TO PONDER

The greatest mistake a person can make is to be afraid of making one.
ELBERT HUBBARD

Failure is only the opportunity to more intelligently begin again.
HENRY FORD

*Because its purpose is to create a customer, the business has
two—and only two—functions: marketing and innovation.
Marketing and innovation produce results. All the rest are costs.*
PETER DRUCKER

It can't be said too many times; the purpose of every business is to find, satisfy and retain customers in a profitable manner. The real value of your business is directly tied to the future, predictable cash flow from your customers/clients. Marketing will help you achieve this critical imperative by allowing you to grow exponentially, instead of incrementally. A strategic business owner takes full advantage of the power and leverage of marketing.

GROWING YOUR BUSINESS

What is marketing? First, it's about deeply understanding the needs and wants of your customers and providing them with greater value. You must clearly identify the demand in the marketplace. At minimum, most businesses can significantly improve in this area. The real power and leverage of marketing comes from the next level of influence: convincingly communicating your unique and superior value proposition.

Marketing is about communicating with and educating your customers, prospects and referral sources as to why it's in their best interests to do business with your company. It is about educating the right target audience on the unique advantages, benefits, values and results you can provide, and sharing the credible evidence/reasons that support these promises. In short, marketing is about educating your target market on the advantages of doing business with you and the reasons why they should trust you to deliver on your promises.

Instead of impacting one prospect at a time (i.e., direct selling), marketing allows you to communicate with and influence many buyers at once. In a sense, marketing is a one-to-many selling system. Marketing allows you to target and influence large groups of customers, prospects, alliances, referral sources, reporters, etc., in a single action.

Unfortunately, most business owners mistakenly try to tackle goals like growing their sales with a one-to-one combat mentality. For example, instead of considering the leverage of marketing (i.e., strategic alliances, referral systems, direct mail, telemarketing, etc.) to grow sales, many owners go for a single weapon, like direct selling. That's their comfort zone—but in reality, it's a deadly rut. They miss the chance to use air support (marketing) to vastly aid their ground war (selling). They fail to explore new options, approaches, or strategies.

While all businesses have a selling process (converting leads to customers), most do not have a legitimate marketing process (generating qualified leads). Consequently, they miss out on tremendous leverage and opportunities.

Your goal should be to add an ongoing marketing process to your business. Again, marketing is nothing more than understanding the needs of your customers and then communicating to them the advantages/benefits they can derive by doing business with you. Think of marketing as continuing education. You are schooling customers, prospects and referral sources on why it's in their best interest to do business with your company.

There are only five ways to grow your business:

1. Keep the customers you have.

2. Bring in more customers.

3. Increase the average transaction size (unit sale).

4. Increase the frequency of purchases.

5. Say "no" to bad customers/prospects.

In short, keep the customers you have while bringing in more, and sell larger amounts more often. Do one of these and your business grows; do two or more of these well and your business can grow by quantum leaps and bounds—exponential growth instead of mere linear growth.

KEEP WHAT YOU HAVE, GROW WHAT YOU HAVE

Don't underestimate the need to satisfy and retain customers. Most businesses put too much money, time and effort into chasing new customers/prospects, but far fewer resources trying to keep their current ones. We all know you can't fill a leaky bucket. Real profits and stable revenue streams come from long-term relationships and repeat business with your current, loyal, profitable customers. Some experts say that 80% of a company's future growth comes from existing clients, if they're served and cultivated properly. That's why customer satisfaction and retention should be your No. 1 marketing priority.

Again, the purpose of a business is to attract and retain customers. You can't grow and remain in business without keeping the customers you currently have. First, you must measure your current attrition rate (loss of customers) and set a goal for dramatically reducing this rate. Let's say, on average, you lose 20% of your customers every year. A realistic goal would be to reduce this attrition rate to 10% per year. Bottom line, it is easier and nearly eight times cheaper to serve and retain current clients/customers than to pursue new ones.

Once you have plugged the holes in your attrition bucket, you want to better serve and get closer to these profitable and worthy customers. You want to better understand their needs, then fulfill as many of these as possible with additional products and services. Continually communicate with your customers. Give them value. Give them solutions. Focus on them and their needs, not on your products/services.

Communicate with them in person, in letters, in faxes, in emails, via your website, brief newsletters, etc. Don't worry—you can't over-communicate with your customers. As you do with your employees, keep them informed, involved and inspired to continue doing business with you. Don't fail to ask your customers these questions:

- How are we doing?

- What other needs do you have?

- How can we improve our value to you?

Your objective is to provide them with more value more frequently; as a result, you will benefit with more profits. Never sell to a customer only once. Real profits come from repeat business. Set goals to increase the frequency and size of repeat business. You want ongoing relationships and ongoing sales.

WINNING NEW CUSTOMERS AND CLIENTS

Bottom line, to be successful at winning new customers and clients, you need to be perceived as being different, special and better. You cannot afford to be viewed as a commodity. Commodity companies are paid commodity prices and fees. There is tremendous power and profit in being perceived as unique, different and better.

Spend time researching and establishing your company's unique selling proposition (USP). What is your most powerful and compelling advantage? What is the greatest benefit of buying your product or service? Why do customers continue to do business with you? What major frustrations do you remove from their lives? Once you define your USP, broadcast it nonstop in your sales presentations, brochures, direct mail, on your website, in your telephone answering methods, in your advertisements and in your news releases. Make that your unique message.

Do not let your USP simply be *quality, service and price*. This says nothing different and has no emotional power. It sounds trite and comes across as "blah, blah, blah" to your prospective customers. Instead, clearly delineate your differences and performance guarantees. Rather than being a mere marketing consultant, be a marketing partner that guarantees revenue results (pay-for-performance) or the client doesn't pay. As a great example, take FedEx's former USP; "when it positively, absolutely needs to be there overnight." That's both clear and unique.

Additionally, to achieve substantial increases in profits and customer satisfaction, you must challenge yourself to come up with new products and services, or repackage old ones in a way that truly excites and delights customers and clients. To qualify as killer ideas and killer solutions, they must include the following:

1. An obvious, compelling **benefit** to the potential buyer

2. Believable **evidence or reasons** that support this benefit (credibility)

3. **A significant difference** from existing products or services (dramatically new and better)

4. A simple and effective means to communicate the benefit, evidence, and difference to the target market

Such killer ideas can revolutionize your business and industry. Dream big!

Bring new marketing strategies into play to attract new customers and clients. Now that you've established how you're different, special, and better than the competition, other ways to draw new clients include...

- **Leverage your past customer relationships.** Revisit with past, worthy customers or inactive customers and express your interest in rekindling the relationship and solving any of their current problems. These folks did business with you once, wrote checks to you, and may be receptive to reactivating their relationship with you; however, you must identify and heal any unresolved wounds and share with them the benefits of doing

MASTERING THE POWER OF MARKETING

business with your company again. Give them an inducement (bonus, discount, additional service level, etc.) for taking action and ordering once again.

- **Formalize and optimize your referral systems.** Identify (crunch numbers, don't rely on hunches) your best-performing referral sources (some use the term market influencers) over the past 12 months and be sure to thank and reward them for their efforts. Communicate with these proven providers often to maintain a top-of-mind awareness. Once you identify these top providers, shamelessly clone these folks. For example, if you are a house painting company and determine that your best referral sources have been real estate agents, replicate this formula. Don't complicate the magic. Educate others as to the specific types of customers and circumstances you serve best. Referral source cultivation is one of the most underutilized, yet low-cost, high-yield marketing weapons that exists.

- **Leverage those relationships that your business helps to financially support** (your banker, CPA, attorney, suppliers, financial adviser, insurance agent, etc.). To determine which would make for good informal sales agents for your business, ask these kinds of questions:

  ▫ Who will benefit from our success as we continue to grow and expand?

  ▫ Who do we write checks to on a regular basis who would have a vested interest in supporting our business development efforts?

Identify these relationships and ask these folks to reciprocate and support your growth efforts through leads, referrals, testimonials, etc.

- **Leverage indirect competitors to gain new customers.** Indirect competitors are companies you seldom go head-to-head with, competing for business. You could establish a formal referral relationship (swap leads, pay finder's fees, share revenue, and do co-marketing) with an indirect competitor that is much larger or smaller than you/or in a different geographic region. For example, a smaller CPA firm could establish an alliance with a large CPA firm and swap leads that don't fit their respective niches. A small, traditional plumbing business could form an alliance with a plumbing company that focuses on doing only the tough, complex, big jobs. Leads could flow both ways.

- **Gain leverage from current clients and customers.** Ask current buyers for introductions and referrals to other potential buyers, or ask current customers to provide endorsements, testimonials, or serve as references. Always ask current clients about any unmet needs they may have.

- **Identify and cultivate complementary businesses as strategic alliances.** For example, a technology consulting firm might want to form alliances with those that can help steer business their way (CPAs, software/hardware vendors, or other non-competitive consultants). To find potential referral or alliance partners, simply ask yourself, "Who already has the trust and respect of our prospects?"

- **Make doing business easy, convenient and risk-free.** Do not ask the other party to assume risk if they start a business relationship with you. Instead, offer them an unconditional, money-back guarantee upfront. Don't keep your guarantee hidden; broadcast it. A credible and specific guarantee will bring in far more business than it costs you. A simple example is, "If you don't find our technology training courses among the best you have ever taken, simply ask for a refund before the start of the second day, and we will gladly return 100% of your money without any questions or delay."

- **Use direct-response advertising.** Don't waste money on ineffective advertising. Always make sure any advertising contains a compelling offer or benefit and motivates the reader, listener or viewer to take action. Never advertise just an image. Advertise only to sell something. Track the effectiveness of your ads to generate leads and/or sales. If the ads don't seem to be working, kill them. Never advertise merely to stroke your ego.

- **Consider using telemarketing.** Use it to develop leads for your salespeople or use telemarketers to follow up a direct mail or advertising campaign. Consider using telemarketing to follow up a sale to see if the person requires any additional help, advice, services or products like warranties, add-on products, or additional levels of service. If you just cleaned the carpet in two rooms of a customer's house, call them in a week to ask if they'd like other rooms in their home to look as good. Offer them a discount as incentive for taking immediate action.

- **Influence many people at once with special events/ seminars.** Consider hosting educational events for customers, referral sources and prospects. Consider holding them in conjunction with other companies (newspapers, radio stations, suppliers, banks, CPA firms, industry experts, trade associations, complementary companies, etc.). This will allow you to tap into their customer relationships. For example, if you are an upscale travel agency introducing new exotic trips, consider co-hosting an event with an upscale radio station or magazine, or with a high-end jewelry store, auto dealership, country club, or money management firm.

- **Consider using direct mail.** Direct mail is simply putting a powerful and complete sales presentation in writing. This vehicle allows you to touch many buyers at once—providing you with immense leverage. Most owners would be best served in the long run by hiring a professional direct marketer on a project basis.

- **Consider using public relations.** Public relations can be a powerful source of leverage as you educate and influence a targeted audience about your benefits, expertise, etc. Get to know the reporters in your industry and periodically call them with some story ideas.

- **Gain leverage by improving the effectiveness of your sales approach.** Give your salespeople a proven, simple sales methodology. For example, use READ.

- ▫ Relate to your prospect.

- ▫ Establish their need or problem.

- ▫ Advance a tailored solution.

- ▫ Determine next steps.

  It's all about building relationships and solving problems. Buy books, tapes, or CDs on selling skills and distribute them to your sales team. Also, periodically send your salespeople to strategic selling courses. Huge payoff!

- **Buy other reputable businesses** possessing great reputations and strong goodwill to gain access to their loyal customers. Be sure their business is a good fit for your company's culture, values, and customer base.

INCREASE THE AMOUNT/FREQUENCY OF PURCHASES

To get your current customers to spend more with your organization, more often, you must increase the "perceived value" of what you offer. Educate your customers so that they'll desire your products and services even more.

To make this happen, you must first increase the collective "self-esteem" of your organization. You and your employees must believe you are better, unique, and highly valuable to your customers, even worth a premium price. You must fight the "we are a commodity" mindset with every fiber of your mind, body and soul. The day you believe you are in a commodity industry or business is the day you begin to die. If you are similar to the others, you must break out from the pack. For example, add more services to your offering; give greater performance and money-back guarantees, provide ongoing education seminars for your buyers or consider packaging or bundling other products or services with yours. Again, find ways to stand out from the crowd and offer greater value than your competitors.

Here are some ideas to increase the average purchase size and frequency of your sales:

- **Raise your prices, if you can.** Educate your buyers on the superior advantages, benefits and results you provide and explain "the reasons why" you need to raise prices—increasing manufacturing costs, customer-service enhancements, better guarantees, better ingredients, etc.

- **Upsell.** If your client/customer can achieve better results and more satisfaction, educate them on buying a higher-end product or service. Do a better job of assessing their needs and matching them to products or services that will give them the optimal buying experience and satisfaction. You will increase your profits and their fulfillment. Auto dealers are masters at getting customers to buy car models with the higher-end feature packages (i.e. leather interior, better stereos, etc.)

- **Cross-sell.** If you have multiple product or service lines, communicate and educate your customers and clients on the full spectrum of your solutions—your range of services, products and expertise. Continually research their challenges and problems and match them up with the solutions you offer. CPA firms, for example, cross-sell their audit clients on tax and consulting services. Banks cross-sell their checking customers on investments, mortgages, lines of credit, and credit cards.

- **Bundle better.** Consider packaging complementary products and services together. If a customer is going to buy a gas grill, for example, offer them a complete package of cooking utensils, mesquite wood chips, barbecue book, grill cover and apron. By saving the customer time and helping them to buy a more "complete solution," you can probably charge a premium for this "barbecue in the box" offering. At the very least, they will have bought more than they otherwise would have—because you made buying easy.

- **Offer volume or frequent buyer discounts.** If you can get your customers to buy more and buy more frequently, reward them—with incentives, discounts, or extra levels of services. Because you have maximized your cash flow, be willing to reward them with a few extra perks. Bookstores and airlines have "frequent buyer" programs. Think of the coffee store or pizza shop that offers you a free serving when you buy a certain number of times.

- **Offer products and services that will complement what you already sell.** Ask the question, "Who else sells something that goes before, after or along with my customer's purchase?" For example, if you sell computer products, consider selling "technical-needs analysis" services on the front-end or installation and computer training services on the back-end. Be sure it makes economic sense to add such services to your business.

- **Communicate with your customers often and give them buying ideas or solutions via mail, phone, email, newsletters, or in-store displays.** If you are a hardware store, you might use direct mail and in-store displays to communicate to your customers the need to fill cracks and seal coat their driveways as fall approaches. Sell them on the benefits of taking such action. Package all the supplies together (sealant, crack filler, broom, gloves, removal cleaner, "how to" booklet, etc.) and offer a single-solution price.

- **Conduct special events to educate your existing customers on your additional service or product offerings.** Do this in an informative manner and in a way that has "their best interests" at heart. Hold a "sneak preview" for your new products, services, models, etc. Hold exclusive events for your best customers. An upscale luxury auto dealer might hold a wine and cheese party with a musical quartet to unveil the newest car models.

- **Endorse other people's products or services to your client list and get a cut of the action.** If, for example, you are an upscale jewelry store, consider offering elaborate vacation packages to your customers via an upscale travel agency. Mail offers to your customer database, endorse the travel agency and their offering, and receive a set percentage of any revenues generated. Instead of adding computer training to your computer store, form an alliance with a reputable training company and negotiate for a "cut of the action" for introducing/ endorsing them to your customers via email, direct mail, telemarketing, etc. To maintain the goodwill of your customers, make sure you do your "due diligence" and introduce only high-trust, high-integrity, high-value organizations to your customer base.

SELECTIVELY SAY "NO"

(Please note; this section contains advice aimed at those who sell primarily to businesses, rather than to the general public.)

To devote more time and attention to your best opportunities and customers, you need to adopt a selective mindset. You can't optimize your business performance if you are constantly bombarded by unprofitable, ungrateful, disagreeable, ever-complaining and energy-draining customers. You and your employees deserve better.

You must learn to say no to prospects who do not fit your profitability profile and goodbye to cheap, unpleasant, unprofitable customers. This single act of firing your problem accounts frees up capacity so you can handle more profitable growth. The 80/20 rule (Pareto Principle) is a helpful guide. This rule says that 80% of your profits come from the top 20% of your customers. Conversely, 80% of your headaches and problems come from the lower 20% of your customer base (the dogs). It is these troublesome 20% that are draining your profits and life force. You need to cut them loose.

Either raise your prices to compensate for the pain and suffering they cause, or flat out fire them. That's right—have the courage to fire those customers that are a real burden to your people and organization. Getting rid of them will free up your people and resources to attract and win superior customers and provide more time, attention and value to your existing quality customers. Your employees and your bottom line will thank you.

As a suggestion, for those serving business entities, separate your customer base into three tiers. Tier 1 customers are your most profitable customers who value, appreciate and regularly buy your offerings. Dedicate the majority of your organization's time and talents into serving Tier 1. Spend slightly less resources on Tier 2 customers, and provide minimal service to Tier 3 customers. Your goals are to develop Tier 2 to become Tier 1 accounts, and to either move your Tier 3 customers up a rung or out the door.

EXPERIMENT LIKE MAD

No matter which strategies you employ, your ultimate leverage comes from focused brainpower—intellectual capital and innovative ideas. Think "brain equity," not "sweat equity." One innovative idea could help your business achieve quantum breakthroughs in performance and results. One innovative idea could significantly multiply your leads generated, revenues, profits, customer satisfaction, quality level and/or competitive advantage. As the leader, you need to encourage practical creativity, experimentation and innovation—the process of asking better questions.

As a CEO, you should be experimenting with new approaches all the time. Encourage your employees to test new strategies, hunches, sales approaches and marketing weapons. Small-scale, controlled testing is critical to optimizing your business and for finding powerful leverage points both within and outside your business. For example, you could test the following:

- A new method of targeting your prospects
- A new sales presentation

- A new direct mail offer or special event
- A new headline in your ads, direct mail campaign or press releases
- A new hiring or retention practice
- A new channel of distribution
- A new strategic alliance
- A new compensation structure
- A new collection method
- A new customer service initiative
- A new referral system
- A new internal communication method

Try many things and implement those that work better than existing approaches. You need to continually listen to your employees, current and former customers, and team of advisors. Ask your internal and external contacts, "How can we improve _____ and get greater results?" If you think your ways or ideas are the best, all new ideas will pass you by. Look outside your industry as well for fresh ways and "killer" ideas. Do not be myopic. Be intellectually and emotionally curious and tuned into your employees, customers, vendors, etc. Keep a small notebook, personal data assistant, or a recorder with you at all times to capture your ideas and hold yourself accountable.

SUGGESTED ACTION ITEMS:

- Marketing is a weapon used by strategic business owners to achieve substantial growth. Commit to marketing. Commit resources.

- Marketing is about educating your target market (current and past customers, prospects, referral sources, and influencers) on the advantages of doing business with your company and the reasons why they should trust you to deliver on your promises. Make "education" and "influence" the focus of your marketing.

- Commit to add a robust marketing process (on-going education) to your business. Your goal is to educate and influence groups of people simultaneously.

- Remember this key concept: There are only five ways to grow your business:

   1. Keep the customers you have.

   2. Bring in more customers.

   3. Increase the average transaction size (unit sale).

   4. Increase the frequency of purchases.

   5. Learn to say "no" to bad customers and prospects.

   Keep the customers you have while bringing in new ones, and sell larger amounts more often. Do one of these and your business grows. Do two or more well, and your business can grow by quantum leaps and bounds; exponential growth instead of mere linear growth.

- **Keep What You Have**
   - Make customer and client retention your No. 1 goal. Measure your current annual attrition rate (loss of customers) and set a goal to cut it in half.

▫ Communicate with and continually educate your current customers on the advantages of your solutions. Use all means necessary: email, mail, phone, in-person, fax, brief newsletters, your website, etc. Learn to better understand their needs and ask them:

1. How are we doing?

2. How can we improve our value to you?

3. What other needs do you have?

- **Attract New Customers**

  ▫ Spend time crafting your unique selling proposition (USP). What makes your business special, different and better? Communicate your competitive advantages like crazy in all you do and say.

  ▫ Come up with killer ideas for your products and services. Remember, to qualify as "killer ideas" and "killer solutions," they need to include the following:

1. An obvious, compelling **benefit** to the potential buyer.

2. Believable **evidence or reasons** that support this benefit (credibility).

3. A **significant difference** from existing products and services (dramatically new and better).

4. A simple and effective means to communicate the benefit, evidence and difference to the target market. Such killer ideas can revolutionize your business and industry. Dream big.

Consider trying three to five of these marketing strategies to gain new customers:

1. Leverage past customer relationships.

2. Formalize and optimize your referral systems.

3. Leverage those relationships that your business helps to financially support (CPAs, bankers, suppliers, etc.).

4. Leverage indirect competitors.

5. Gain leads and referrals from current customers and clients.

6. Identify and cultivate complementary businesses as strategic alliances.

7. Make doing business with you easy, convenient, fun and risk-free.

8. Only use direct-response advertising, not image advertising.

9. Investigate the utilization of telemarketing.

10. Use special events/seminars to influence groups of people.

11. Consider using direct marketing.

12. Consider public relations.

13. Improve the effectiveness of your company's sales approach/process.

14. Buy out other reputable and complementary businesses to gain their clients.

- **Get customers to increase the amount and frequency of purchases by implementing three to five of these strategies:**

  - Increase the collective "self-esteem" of your organization—fight the "we are a commodity" mindset.

  - Raise your prices and explain why.

  - Upsell.

  - Cross-sell.

  - Bundle your solutions (products and services) better.

  - Offer volume or frequent buyer incentives.

  - Offer other products/services that complement what you currently sell.

  - Communicate with your customers often and give them "opportunities" to buy.

  - Conduct special events to educate current customers on your additional offerings.

  - Endorse other people's products/services to your clients for a cut of the action.

- **Learn to say "no" to unprofitable customers/prospects:**

  - Learn to say no to unworthy prospects and unprofitable customers. Fire your "dog" accounts. Use the 80/20 rule as a guide

  - Consider separating customers into a Tier System. Put most of your time and effort into serving your Tier 1 and Tier 2 accounts. Move Tier 3 up to the next rung, or out the door

- **Experiment Like Mad**
  - As CEO, make sure your employees are continually asking questions like "How can we improve _____ and get better results?"
  - Test current marketing strategies and approaches against new ones. Keep those that work better, lose those that don't.
  - Encourage experimentation—drive out fear.
  - Look outside your business and industry for better ways to do things.

CHAPTER 9

STRATEGIC RELEASE— LEARNING TO LET GO

POINTS TO PONDER

You never achieve real success unless you like what you are doing.
– DALE CARNEGIE

There is only one success—to be able to
spend your life in your own way.
– CHRISTOPHER MORLEY

He is a wise man who does not grieve for the things which
he has not, but rejoices for those which he has.
– EPICTETUS

After the first few years of business ownership, reality sets in. For most owners, the initial joy of "doing your own thing" has faded. Your supposed ticket to freedom has turned into a sentence of servitude. Your "baby" has become a "rotten kid." What was once a very exciting mission has turned into the daily grind. Your American Dream now seems to be an unattainable fairytale.

Just because you own a business does not mean you must forego a fulfilling and active personal life. Quite the contrary;

your business should be a tool to help you get more out of life, not less. A business should free you up, not tie you down.

If you have implemented the strategic business owner concepts discussed (thinking and acting like a CEO; systematizing and documenting the business; leading, planning, and managing your people and marketing), then letting go of the day-to-day and hour-to-hour operations of the business should be doable.

YOU ARE NOT YOUR BUSINESS

In order to build a systems-dependent business that functions without you, you must think of yourself as separate from the business. You are not your business and your business is not you. View your business as a means to an end; a tool to help you create more fulfillment, freedom, wealth and options.

To let go and escape the tyranny of the details, you cannot be emotionally welded to the business. You are a worthwhile human being with or without your business. Do not let your ego, self-worth and self-esteem be tied up with the business. The business is but one facet of your life, and while it is a very important component, it is not the end all. It should not fully define who you are.

Your value and worth as a human being are separate from the value of your business. You must not take your business too seriously. Odds are, you are not curing cancer. While whatever you are doing is important, it is not more important than your family and friends, your health, your faith, your fulfillment and your joy in life.

The time, attention and love you share with your spouse, family, kids or friends are much more important to them than your title, or how much money you make. While you can always make more money, you cannot make more time or replay life. You do not get another chance to be a spouse, family member, or friend. This is not a dress rehearsal. Get your priorities in order now!

Keep things in perspective. No matter how bad things get, never forget you have options. You can walk away from the business, sell it to someone else, or hire a professional business manager (chief operating officer) to handle the day-to-day issues. Worst case, you can always get a job! Knowing you have choices should prevent you from ever feeling totally trapped by or dependent on your business.

Before you can satisfy your employees, customers, investors and business partners, you must first satisfy yourself with the business. It must serve your needs and wants over the long haul. If you don't stay in the game long enough, you do no one any good. There should be joy in being a business owner. Learn to let go. Trust your business system and trust your people.

ACKNOWLEDGE DEATH

Bad news; no matter how hard you work or how much money you make, you will not live forever. Even as you read this, your time is running out. You cannot save time, invest it or buy more of it; you can only "spend" it. How wisely are you spending your time?

Be brave and be aware of you own mortality. Face reality; you have a limited time on earth. By acknowledging the fact of your eventual death, life becomes sweeter, more meaningful and more precious. By facing death head on, you are liberated to live life fully. Realizing that life is finite, you make wiser choices, especially about how, where and with whom you spend time.

Do a quick test; it's called the tombstone test. Draw a tombstone and include your birth date, a dash, and your best guess for a death date. Do the math; determine the years you most likely have left. Now ask yourself...

- What do I want written on my tombstone?
- How do I want to be remembered?
- What's my legacy?
- What really matters most to me?

Odds are, you want to be remembered as a good spouse, parent, friend, and provider; a person of good character, a caring leader, follower of your faith, or for making a certain contribution to society.

Does your present way of living match your desired epitaph? Any regrets? Are you leading the type of life for which you want to be remembered? No one on his deathbed wishes he had worked more hours, earned more money, or bought more stuff. Shift your focus on your faith, family, friends and leaving a legacy.

Stop living life reactively, letting urgent yet unimportant matters dictate your days. Face death and live your remaining years the way you truly want to, based on what is most important to you. What do you want to do before you die?

ALL IN THE FAMILY

For many of you, you are also struggling to balance running a business with raising a family and nurturing a marriage or significant relationship. As a result, you are exhausted from treading water in a sea of multiple responsibilities, obligations and expectations. Not surprisingly, divorce rates of entrepreneurs are very high. Beat the odds by talking to your spouse or significant other about your business, your highs and lows, dreams, fears, challenges and feelings. Don't build a business at the cost of your marriage or other key relationships. Stop being a Lone Ranger. Stop suffering in a silent shroud of secrecy. Again, share this book and your feelings with your spouse or significant other. Let them better understand your situation so that they can help you, support you and challenge you.

While on the subject of relationships, be sure to schedule one-on-one time with your family members each week and schedule dates with your spouse/significant other at least twice a month. Running a business is both time- and attention-consuming. Fight this trap. Allow for sufficient time and energy to be an engaged spouse, parent and/or friend.

DEFINE YOUR LIFE

Want more life? Start by making a shift in your mindset. Begin now to set a goal to work less, make more, and have a bigger life. These are achievable goals. To be truly fulfilled, you cannot be focused solely on financial goals. Set personal goals to have more fulfillment, balance and joy in your life. Fulfillment is an inside game. Examine your heart, and know what you truly want. According to Socrates, "The unexamined life is not worth living."

While you probably have a vision for your business, you most likely don't have one for your personal life. Without a personal vision or game plan, your personal life will always be an afterthought, haphazardly conducted and emotionally chaotic. If you fail to plan, you're planning to fail in your personal arena. Work on your life. Be proactive, not reactive.

Know who you are and what you want. Don't live your life based on the expectations of others. Success is getting what you want; happiness is wanting what you get. Now is the time to stop whining and complaining. It's time to create the life you want. You must decide your heart's desires; no one can do this but you. You get to invent your life and set the terms and conditions. Who and what are most important to you? What do you want your personal life to look and feel like in one year, three years, and five years? Once you know what you want, be true to yourself and live the life you want, not what others want.

Begin by asking many questions:

- What's most important to me in life?

- In my heart, gut and soul, what do I truly want for my life?

- What don't I want?

- What are my deepest values (emotional states you desire most)?

- How do I want to spend my remaining time on earth?

- What activities do I want to participate in?

- What relationships are critical to a fulfilling life?

- Where is my life out of balance?

- What do I want to do with my greater freedom and personal time once I function as a strategic business owner?

- What relationships am I failing to nurture and develop?

- If I knew I had only six months to live, what would I change? What would I focus on?

And, please, never confuse "things" with "values." For example, no one really values money itself (a "means" value). Rather, people value money for what it represents or fulfills on an emotional level (an "end" value)—freedom, security, power, accomplishment, etc.

But real fulfillment comes from the deep connections we make with other people and our faith on an emotional and spiritual level. The answer to fulfillment is not more money or bigger and better toys. Money, new cars, houses, clothes and jewelry will not fill in the empty holes in your soul. Only by living a life in alignment with your core values will you experience deep fulfillment, joy, balance and happiness. In order to avoid burnout, you must consistently make and take time to renew and refresh your battery.

GET HELP LETTING GO

Giving up day-to-day control of a business is hard. Letting go of the reins can be scary. Delegating can be a challenge; however, if you're going to have more life and greater personal fulfillment, you cannot keep doing it all. Quit being a micro-manager or control freak. You must yield control to gain freedom.

It's physically impossible to manage every aspect of a business. You must trust your people and the planning, procedures and policies you have put in place. Reluctance to trust and rely on others is a weakness, not a strength. Trust the integrated business system you created.

If you haven't done so already, get a business coach who will help you to:

- Become a strategic business owner.

- Work **on** your business instead of **in** your business.

- Focus more on tomorrow and less on today.

- Tackle important matters, not urgent matters.

- See and face reality (your repeated, external behavior), rather than depending on your flawed, myopic internal perceptions.

- Think and act like a CEO, not a front-line employee.

- Put business systems in place to replace you.

- Lead your team and leverage your opportunities.

- Create a simple business plan.

- Set personal and business goals and keep youself accountable for reaching them.

If you do not want a personal coach, ask one of your advisers to serve this critical role.

Again, if you can't keep out of the details or if you are not focusing on your areas of brilliance, think about bringing in a professional manager or executive. Consider hiring a president or chief operating officer to handle the day-to-day issues of the business while you focus on the more strategic areas.

VALUE YOUR TIME MORE THAN MONEY

Broaden your definition of wealth. Wealth is more than just money. Real wealth is about physical and mental health, close relationships, and emotional and spiritual wellbeing, to name a few of its components. You can have lots of money, yet still be lonely and emotionally bankrupt.

After all, you can always make more money, but you can't make more time. How much money do you really need? How much is enough? Time should have much more value and importance to you than money. Again, what do you want to do with your personal time? What's most important to you? To have fulfillment, you must choose how best to spend your time.

Do not confuse busyness with productivity. Don't confuse activity with accomplishment. Always ask, "What is the highest and best use of my time?" Focus on "what and why" and less on "how." Use the 80/20 rule to your advantage. What 20% of your talents, skills and experiences will give your company the greatest return? What 20% of the organization can you focus on to yield the greatest bottom-line results? You should never have to work more than 9-10 hours per day, especially after a few years in the business. If you do, you are working hard, but not working smart. Change the mindset—long hours don't necessarily equal success.

Stop trying to manage every second of every day. Start managing important relationships, both inside and outside the company. Focus on those individuals you need to spend time with, those that need your love, attention and mentoring. Focus on people and priorities.

BARRIERS TO CHANGE—BE AWARE

Why do so few owners embrace new ways of running their businesses? Why is there such resistance to change? In brief, here are some of the more common barriers to healthy change:

- Many entrepreneurs are more comfortable with old problems and beliefs than with crafting new solutions. They prefer the known to the unknown. Inertia and complacency have set in. Some are too shortsighted. They're not willing to endure short-term sacrifice and discomfort to create long-term benefits. This is similar to people struggling to quit smoking, lose weight, begin exercising, etc. The avoidance of short-term pain is greater motivation than the desire for long-term pleasure and benefits.

- Owners are prisoners to their habits and frames of mind. They simply "fly by the seats of their pants," and default to what they know best. They are handcuffed by their paradigms (mental pattern for seeing their environment), technical expertise and comfort zone.

- Some owners have bought into the deadly myth that business ownership requires exceptionally long hours, tough days and much sacrifice. While this may be necessary starting out, they should not commit themselves to a life sentence of hard time. But they do! They believe deeply the "no pain, no gain" motto and quietly and secretly suffer through the blues. There is even a prejudice that "thinking, planning and leading" are not meaningful activities. Instead, they put on their work boots and try working even harder. They wade even deeper into the details. They get busy being busy. They "just do it." But instead of satisfaction and security, such self-delusions bring pain, suffering and bondage.

- Some owners are convinced they have all the answers and are not receptive to challenging old assumptions or considering new ideas that could substantially improve their businesses and lives. They waste precious energy defending what they know for sure. Little can be done to help these folks. They are not coachable.

- The most overwhelming barrier to change is most owners are too busy to slow down, reflect and set a new course. As a result, they never escape the daily "fire drills" long enough to think about and implement better strategies. When you're surrounded by smoke, you cannot see the big picture and big changes that need to take place to improve your business and your life. Instead, you instinctively and reactively tackle low-priority, high-urgency tasks. Use this book as your forced reflection.

You must accept that, with help, you can overcome most of these barriers. In fact, consider them convenient excuses. Identify which of these barriers is your favorite excuse for not taking action. Commit to kill this excuse and overcome inertia. Engage your coach in the process.

OTHER SUGGESTIONS FOR HAPPINESS

- Don't try to be better than others; simply try to be the best you can be.

- Don't compare yourself to others; someone will always possess something to a greater degree.

- Magnify your blessings; focus on what you already have, not what you don't have.

- See life through a lens of abundance, not of scarcity; others don't have to lose for you to win.

- Live the life you want, not the life others want for you.

- Live by design, not by default.

- Stop seeking happiness in the wrong place; it is not found in things.

- Keep learning as if you were immortal, but live life fully realizing that you are not.

- Don't seek visible things as much as invisible things.

- Change what you must; accept what you can't change.

SUGGESTED ACTION ITEMS:

- Realize you are not the business and the business is not you. It is a separate entity. Your value as a human being is separate from the value of your business.

- Acknowledge your mortality. When you face death, you can truly begin to live life. Remember what you want on your tombstone and live your life accordingly. Do not live according to the expectations of others—it's your life.

- If you are married or have a significant other in your life, make sure they read this book once you've finished it. Give them a thirty-day window in which to complete it. To understand you and your situation better, they need to appreciate your world and your challenges more fully. Given a common foundation of understanding, there can be more frequent and open communication and richer collaboration. Do not try to be a silent, stoic, Lone Ranger any more.

- Ask your spouse or significant other to provide you with continual feedback on your progress at home. Over time, they should sense a more relaxed, engaged and joyful spouse, parent and friend.

- Winning at business, but losing at home is not success. A balanced and fulfilling life is success. Therefore, schedule family time each week. Plan for and spend unencumbered time with your family members throughout the week and give them your undivided time, love and attention.

- Plan and schedule two dates a month with your spouse or significant other.

- Again, insist your spouse or significant other and key business advisers read this book. They can't help you unless they understand your challenges and the solutions.

- Get a life. Get a vision for your personal life. In the same spirit in which you've designed your business vision, design the type of life you want to live. Share this with your coach and your spouse/significant other. Know what is most important to you and shape your life accordingly.

- Use your coach to help you let go. If you can't let go and get out of the details, hire a professional business manager.

- You can always make more money, but you can't make more time. Time should have much more value and importance to you. Stop trying to manage your time. Start managing important relationships, both inside and outside the company. Focus on those individuals you need to spend time with, those who need your love, attention and mentoring.

- Before doing a task, ask, "Does this task lead directly to increased profits, significantly reduced costs, improved customer satisfaction, or to me building a better business"? If it doesn't, dismiss the task or delegate it.

- Again, do those things only you can do as CEO and delegate the rest. You need to free up time to do CEO activities that make your business and personal vision a reality.

- Admit to yourself that you have habits, comfort zones and paradigms (mental models) that are holding you back. Set a goal to discover and confront these mental beasts. Share these barriers with your coach and spouse/significant other so they can be on the lookout for them. See these barriers as excuses that can be overcome with the strategies in this book and with the help of your accountability team.

- Choose to live a life by design, not by default!

SOME FINAL POINTS TO PONDER

Thinking is the hardest work there is. That is why so few people engage in it.
HENRY FORD

It's what you learn after you know it all that counts.
JOHN WOODEN

The art of being wise is the art of knowing what to overlook.
WILLIAM JAMES

CHAPTER 10

CONCLUDING REMARKS

It's time to begin building a better business, a better you, and a better life. It's time to re-shape your thoughts and philosophies. It's time to put joy back into your life and into owning a business. It's time for you to rekindle the fire, passion, excitement and joy of owning a business.

Yes, you *can* work less, earn more, and have greater freedom and fulfillment. This book showed you how. Realize it's the mental game that matters most. Change your mental models and maps and you move in the right direction with far less effort and pain. Again, it's all about shifting mindsets, not shifting gears. Be open to a between-the-ears makeover. The right habits and strategies are much more important than the right tactics. This book has been about mentally adopting the right strategies and attitudes.

Did you get a coach to help you transform? If not, you will not achieve optimal success and happiness. Get a coach on your side, helping you to work "on" yourself, "on" your business, "on" your life, and "on" your dreams and goals.

To refresh your memory, here is the process to greater freedom, fortune and fulfillment—the way to work less and make more by working smarter, not harder.

- **Step One:** Learn to work **on** yourself by transitioning to a new way of thinking and behaving. Re-program yourself and your habits. Stop acting like an employee and start thinking like a CEO. Learn to work **on** your business, not **in** your business. Adopt the theory of optimization. Be strategic, not tactical; work less, lead more!

- **Step Two:** Systematize your company by creating, documenting and continually improving all your key processes, procedures and policies. Trust the business system and personnel you implement and remove yourself from the company's daily details. Be more hands-off and more brains-on. Replace yourself with other people. Define and document the work to be done. Train others and delegate the work. This operating system is your foundation for freedom.

- **Step Three:** Increase your leadership capabilities. Excel at leadership, not doer-ship. Your business needs a clear vision and a strong leader to hold others accountable, not another employee doing technical work. Help build and direct your team.

- **Step Four:** Develop clarity of direction for your business and employees by creating a simple business plan and an effective implementation process.

- **Step Five:** Learn to effectively manage your people, because they're your greatest asset.

- **Step Six:** Instead of incremental growth, engage the leverage of marketing to achieve substantial, profitable growth.

- **Step Seven:** Learn to let go, delegate, and truly enjoy business ownership and your life.

Success is getting what you want; happiness is wanting what you get. You are the author and architect of your business and life. You alone are responsible for designing your business life and personal life. Make sure you design them to work for you and to fulfill your desires, so that you can enjoy both happiness and success.

The key to successful and happy business ownership is to transform your mind. You must start thinking and acting like a CEO, not an employee. If you start leading and better leveraging your time, talent and resources, you will be happier with your business, your life and your results.

Now, go work "on" your business and "on" your personal life.

Wishing you and your business the best.

DANIEL M. MURPHY   **GEORGE MAABADI**

"Enhancing the strategic mindset, focus and results of small business owners, franchisees, managers and the self-employed."

Owning and running a business, done right, should be about generating significant money, freedom and fun. Are you on track? If not, please get some help.

The Growth Coach® is North America's leader in business coaching. Our professionally trained and certified business coaches are located throughout the United States, Canada and Ecuador. They understand deeply the philosophy, strategies, mindsets and process described briefly in this book. They are also certified in The Strategic Mindset® Process, a year-round coaching and accountability process that helps business owners to achieve greater focus, freedom and financial success. You can locate a business coach near you by visiting www.TheGrowthCoach.com.

The Strategic Mindset® Process is a proven and guaranteed strategic-focusing process that has been helping entrepreneurs for over a decade. Clients participate in unique personal strategic retreats one day every quarter to help achieve greater success and balance in their lives. They discover personal and business management strategies and mindsets that are practical and highly effective. Clients begin to slow down, reflect, face reality and decide on the critical changes necessary to improve their businesses and lives. They come away from each session armed with a 90-day strategic plan, as well as greater clarity and confidence about achieving their vision, strategies and goals.

In addition to quarterly group coaching, Growth Coach® professionals can also deliver one-on-one coaching, tele-coaching, management team development, sales team coaching and special project assistance. All services come with a unique, no-hassle, money-back guarantee.

Printed in the USA
CPSIA information can be obtained
at www.ICGtesting.com
JSHW012053140824
68134JS00035B/3406

9 781599 325750